Santa Fe

an intimate view

Bill Jamison

Milagro Press

Printed in the United States of America

Research and publication assistance: Cheryl Alters
Photos: Cover: Mark Nohl
Page 4 Bill Jamison
Page 34 Bill Jamison
Page 98 Mark Nohl

Design: Chris Nater & Associates
Production: Land O'Sun Printers

ISBN 0-9608504-0-6

Published by
Milagro Press, Inc., P.O. Box 1804,
Santa Fe, New Mexico 87501

Contents

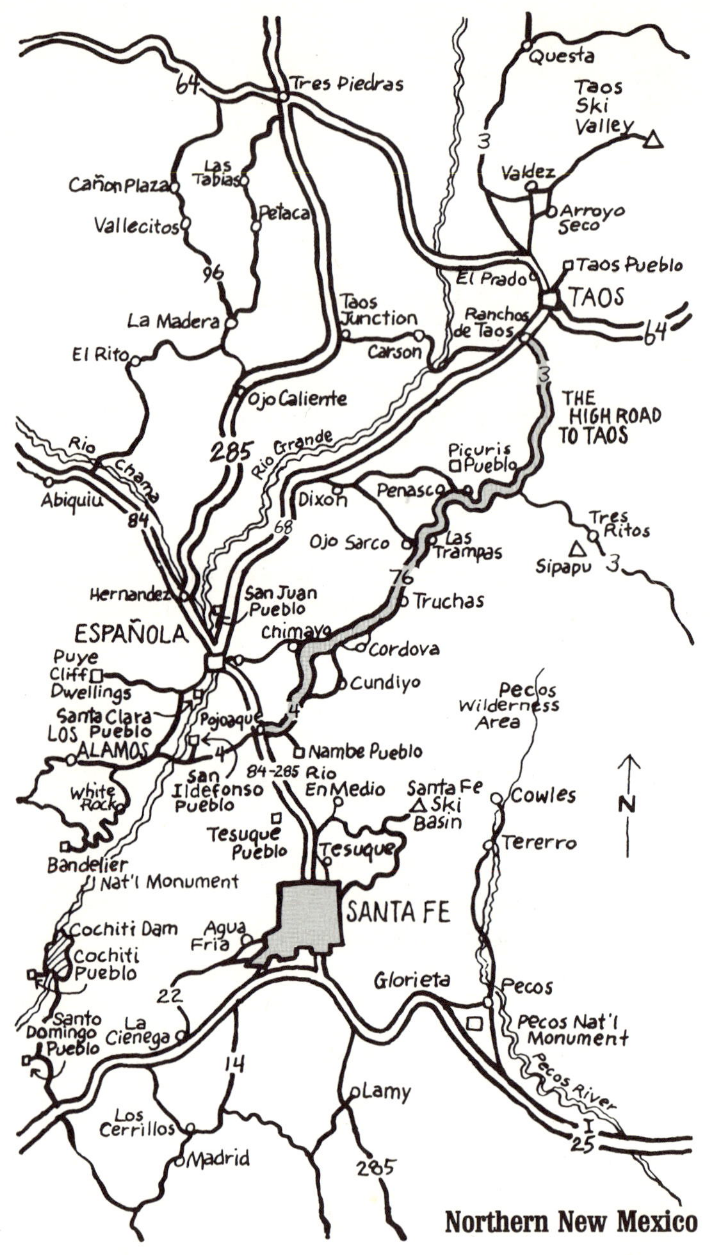
Questa
Taos
Ski
Valley
Tres Piedras
64
3
Valdez
Arroyo
Seco
Las
Tabias
Cañon Plaza
Petaca
Vallecitos
96
Taos Pueblo
El Prado
TAOS
Taos
Junction
Ranchos
de Taos
64
La Madera
Carson
El Rito
3
Ojo Caliente
THE
HIGH ROAD
TO TAOS
Rio Grande
285
Picuris
Pueblo
Rio
Chama
Penasco
Dixon
Abiquiu
84
68
Tres
Ritos
Ojo Sarco
Las
Trampas
Sipapu
3
76
Truchas
Hernandez
San Juan
Pueblo
ESPAÑOLA
Chimayo
Cordova
Puye
Cliff
Dwellings
Cundiyo
Pecos
Wilderness
Area
Santa Clara
Pueblo
LOS
ALAMOS
Pojoaque
4
4
Nambe Pueblo
84-285
Rio
En Medio
San
Ildefonso
Pueblo
White
Rock
Santa Fe
Ski
Basin
Cowles
N
Tesuque
Pueblo
Tesuque
Tererro
Bandelier
Nat'l Monument
SANTA FE
Cochiti Dam
Agua
Fria
Cochiti
Pueblo
Glorieta
Pecos
22
Santo
Domingo
Pueblo
La
Cienega
Pecos Nat'l
Monument
14
Pecos River
Lamy
Los
Cerrillos
I
25
Madrid
285
Northern New Mexico

Santa Fe

Santa Fe Opera
Bishop's Lodge
84-285
Old Taos Hwy.
Bishop's Lodge Rd.
To Santa Fe Ski Basin
Hyde Park Rd.
Paseo de Peralta
PLAZA
Alameda St.
Palace Ave.
Santa Fe River
Canyon Rd.
Cerrillos Rd.
N
Old Santa Fe Trail
Old Pecos Trail
to I-25
St. Michael's Drive
St. Francis Drive
to I-25
Zia Rd.

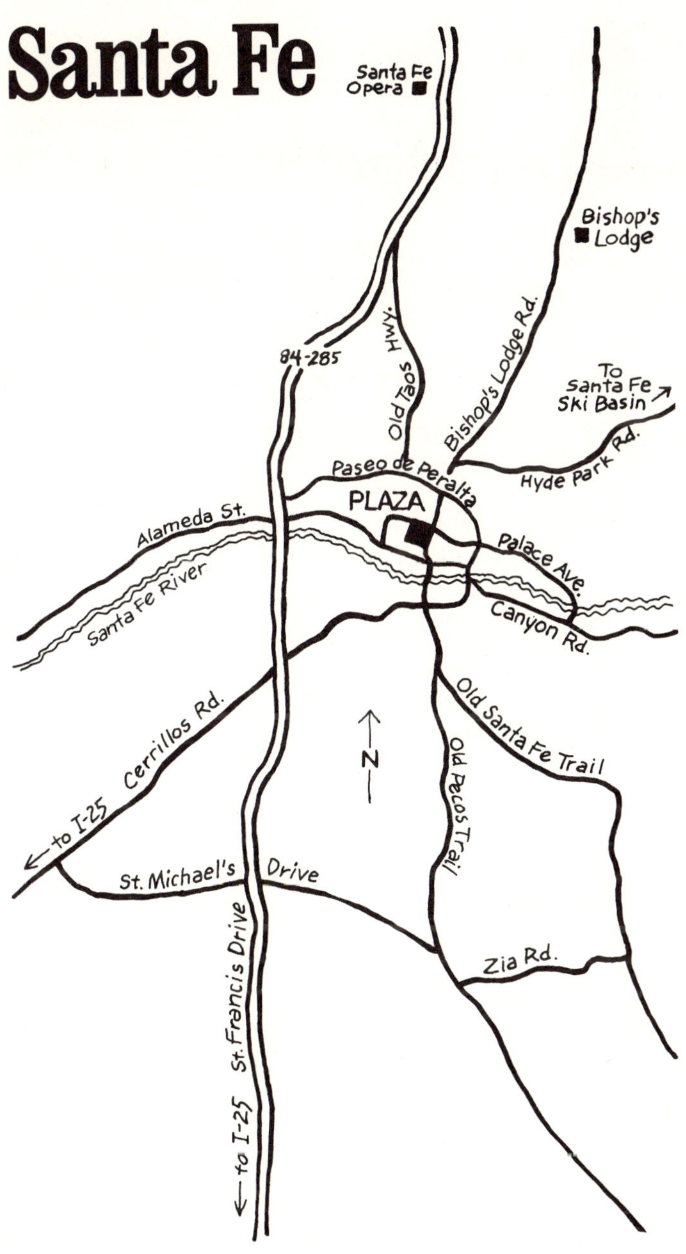

Introduction

Every September most of Santa Fe participates in a pagan spectacle initiated early this century by a leader of the local art colony. The assembled citizenry enthusiastically burns a 40-foot-tall puppet named Zozobra, representing Old Man Gloom. The puppet, pictured on the front cover, flails his arms and groans horribly while the town torches him in an enormous fireworks display. The event dispels gloom from the city and opens the annual Fiesta de Santa Fe.

The Fiesta ends two days later. Many of the same people who burned Zozobra gather in the Cathedral at dusk. After mass they form a long candlelight procession which winds its way slowly up a nearby hill. The procession stops at the top of the hill, by the Cross of the Martyrs, and sings in homage to Franciscan priests killed by Indians in revolt 300 years ago.

The Fiesta is the essence of Santa Fe. The full community joins together every year in dramatic folk pageants, inspired by *Conquistadores* and artists, to celebrate the city's unique and splendid fusion of cultural traditions.

This is not, unfortunately, the Santa Fe being touted recently to the rest of the world. The national media and other trend-setters have been promoting the city lately as a fashionable place for modern quests. *Esquire* discovered it, in a big cover story, to be the new "in" spot for seekers of the vogue. *U.S. News and World Report* claimed that it has "desert chic." *Time* and *Newsweek* both labeled the city a new Salzburg, somehow ignoring the lack of any similarity between

Austrian and Spanish cultures since the dissolution of the Habsburg Empire. Lord and Taylor and Saks Fifth Avenue promoted "the Santa Fe look" in fashions that local residents wouldn't wear. The Washington *Post*, pursuing these confusions to the summit, ranked the city number one in a list of the 25 "in" places of the world.

Anyone attracted to Santa Fe by this hype will be disappointed. Chic cannot be maintained inside mud walls. Spanish colonial customs, Pueblo Indian endurance, and artistic retreat from the mainstream are Santa Fe's foundations, a heritage not likely to form the wave of the future.

This book is about the genuine Santa Fe, incredibly fascinating in the homogenized world of the mass media, but not trendy. A current and comprehensive description of the city, it is intended to serve both as a guide for visitors and as a reference for residents of the area who want to explore Santa Fe fully.

Part One is about the origins and development of the city's distinctive character. The influence of the magnificent natural setting, the persistence of Pueblo and Spanish values, and the impact of the American occupation and the Anglo art colony are depicted in a sweeping but succinct chronicle of Santa Fe's background.

The second section deals with Santa Fe as a living museum. It opens with three walks around old areas of the city, strongly recommended for visitors as basic orientation. Other chapters point out a multitude of places and events, some neglected even by residents, which are vital and impressive aspects of the indigenous heritage.

Part Three provides short descriptions and quality ratings of Santa Fe's restaurants, galleries and shops, hotels, and night spots. The best of these establishments reflect the excitement and lure of the city's traditions as powerfully as the historic, cultural, and natural sights. The book is the only comprehensive source of information about these places not based on advertising in any way.

The overall purpose is to survey Santa Fe's inner substance in its various manifestations, as an introduction for visitors and as a resource for area residents. The trend-setters will soon move on to Scottsdale for desert chic and Ralph Lauren will replace the Santa Fe look with the Seattle look. Nothing will be lost. The city will remain as vibrant and fascinating as before, its fate shaped by a unique combination of deeply-entrenched cultures, not by outside fads. The residents will continue to dispel gloom annually and make the slow candlelight walk to the Cross of the Martyrs. This is the city described here, where the people love to burn Zozobra but would never let him die.

Part One
The essence

Dancing ground of the sun

The Pueblo Indians had a village on the site of Santa Fe six or seven centuries ago, abandoned before the Spanish arrived. In a splendid description of the natural setting, the Pueblos called the place, according to legend, "the dancing ground of the sun."

Though Santa Fe is small — about 50,000 in population today — its natural surroundings are immense. Approaching the city from the south, the vast Southwestern desert gradually and reluctantly yields to the forested peaks of the Jemez Mountains on the west and the Sangre de Cristo Mountains on the east. The town was built along a mountain stream, the Santa Fe River, on a 7,000-foot plateau situated right under the towering shelter of the eastern range. The large sky overhead dominates the perspective. The desert below, like a great ocean, takes an infinity to reach the horizon. The mountains above, and those beyond in all directions, are equally awesome in their massiveness and indifference to people. The Spanish wanted the view primarily for protection against invaders, but it couldn't have escaped the notice of their priests that the sin of human pride, hubris, would be hard to maintain in such a landscape.

Many writers have tried to find language that would match the grandeur of the scenery. One of the noblest failures came from D.H. Lawrence, who lived north of Santa Fe, near Taos, in the 1920s. "For greatness of beauty I have never experienced anything like New Mexico. All those mornings when I went with a hoe along the ditch to the *Canon*, at the ranch, and stood, in the fierce, proud silence of the Rockies, on their foothills, to look far over the desert to the blue mountains away in Arizona, blue as Chalcedony, with the sage-brush desert sweeping grey-blue in between, dotted with tiny cube-crystals of houses, the vast amphitheater of lofty, indomitable desert, sweeping round to the ponderous Sangre de Cristo Mountains on the east, and coming up flush at the pine-dotted foothills of the Rockies! What splendour!"

The land is a magnificent stage for the dazzling performance of the sun. When Lawrence tried to describe the place of the sun in the local environment, he strained even further for an apt image. "Never is the light more pure and overweening as there, arching with a royalty almost cruel over the hollow, uptilted world. It is so easy to understand that the Aztecs gave hearts of men to the sun. For the sun is not merely hot or scorching, not at all. It is of a brilliant and unchallengeable purity and haughty serenity which would make one sacrifice the heart to it. Ah, yes, in New Mexico the heart is sacrificed to the sun and the human being is left stark, heartless, but undauntedly religious."

The sun's intensity in the area is due to a combination of circumstances. Its warmth, which contrasts with the coolness of the mountain air, results from Santa Fe's southern exposure, on the same latitude as Atlanta. The sun's brightness comes from the clarity of the air. At Santa Fe's altitude its rays avoid the last mile and a half of the earth's dust-laden atmosphere. The desert aridity keeps the humidity low and the air relatively free of the misting effect of water particles. The size of the town and its lack of industry preclude serious air pollution. These factors combine to give the sun more rein that it has anywhere else in the United States.

It's the play of the sun and its shadow on mountain, desert, and adobe that has lured so many artists to the area. Robert Henri and

Marsden Hartley, who spent months in Santa Fe on several different visits, were fascinated with the brilliance of the color. Hartley said the area, "is of course the only place in America where true color exists, excepting the short autumnal season in New England." John Sloan, a leading figure in the "ashcan school" of American art, made a summer home where there were no ashcans, just off Canyon Road. His subject matter shifted to the local population, but what was most notable in his work was the shimmering glow of the sun. Andrew Dasburg, probably the greatest of the American cubists, moved permanently to Santa Fe and then Taos. Dasburg said, "I felt as though I had come upon the Garden of Eden; everything was pristine."

The first people to appreciate the amplitude of the place, long before the artists arrived, were those who called it "the dancing ground of the sun." In the complex pantheistic beliefs of the Pueblo peoples, their natural surroundings assume sacred dimensions. Everything, animate and inanimate, has a spirit, which is benevolent or malevolent depending on human respect.

The Pueblos regard the mountains and mesas of the region as the home of their gods, as the Greeks treated Mt. Olympus. The particular formations that are sacred vary among the villages according to what is most prominent locally, but almost all of the major peaks in the Santa Fe area have special religious significance to one village or another. These mountains not only house deities, who are angered by inappropriate intrusions, but also contain sacred lakes and ponds, and are generally associated with compass directions and colors that have important religious significance of their own. Deities also live on some of the mesas in the region, usually ones that are dark and foreboding; they are thought to have dangerous caves where people can disappear from the sun forever.

Most succeeding settlers after the Pueblos were less concerned about their religious harmony with the environment than with its uses. The Spanish wanted the mountains to yield gold and the Americans looked to them for furs, coal, timber, and now uranium. But most residents, and visitors, too, have felt something of the spiritual power that the Pueblos attribute to their land. D.H. Lawrence is not a very representative case for much of anything, but many new arrivals do share his first impression of the place. He came to the area after years of traveling the world, jaded by the expectation of monotony.

"Superficially, the world has become small and known. Poor little globe of earth, the tourists trot round you as easily as they trot round the Bois or round Central Park. There is no mystery left, we've been there, we've seen it, we know all about it.

We are mistaken. I realized this with shattering force when I went to New Mexico. The moment I saw the brilliant, proud morning shine high up over the deserts of Santa Fe, something stood still in my soul and I started to attend. In the magnificent fierce morning of New Mexico one sprang awake, a new part of the soul woke up suddenly, and the old world gave way to a new."*

* The D.H. Lawrence quotes are from *Phoenix; The Posthumous Papers, 1936*, published by Penguin Books.

The Pueblo heritage

The ancestors of the Pueblos, the Anasazi people, settled in the Southwest several thousand years ago, but no one is certain of their origins. The Pueblo explanation is the most interesting. They believe their ancestors came from an underworld beneath the earth's surface, a place that was dark, ugly, and damp, the very opposite of the Southwest. They struggled to climb out and, after many vicissitudes, finally emerged through the earth's navel, onto the land and into the light. The point of emergence is represented by the small opening, or *sipapu*, in Pueblo *kivas*, their sacred ceremonial chambers.

The Anasazi were nomadic hunters and gatherers until they began cultivating corn, about 2000 B.C. Archaeologists have unearthed hundreds of tiny cobs from that ancient period, as thin as a pencil and less than two inches in length. Over the next millennium the Anasazi refined their agricultural methods, added the protein of the bean to their repertory, and learned how to support cities from their farms. In their first permanent settlements, the Anasazi lived in pit houses, large holes in the ground covered with logs. They developed these circular, underground structures originally as granaries for storing corn, but later found them suitable for housing as well.

The Pueblos have never forgotten the importance of corn in the development of their civilization. They use corn meal and pollen as Catholics use holy water, to bless the newborn and the dead and to prepare for important rituals, and they celebrate its spiritual power in some of their most striking ceremonial dances. Their underground *kivas* have remained very similar in structure to the original corn granaries, long after their ancestors began building houses above ground.

The Anasazi were impressive architects. After leaving their pit houses, about the time that Europe was entering the Dark Ages, they constructed some magnificent cities. One of the oldest was in Chaco Canyon, a dry, hot valley in the desert canyonlands of northwestern New Mexico. In their prime, in the 12th century, the Chaco residents built eight large stone structures capable of housing at least 5000 people. Pueblo Bonito, the grandest of these communal dwellings, was four stories high and contained 800 rooms and 30 kivas. It was the largest housing structure built in the Western hemisphere until a New York City landlord topped it in the 1880s. The 40-foot-high walls, some of which are still standing, had to be massive at the base to support the building, but the Anasazi laid the stones with delicate and intricate artistry, as effectively as any modern mason could with much more sophisticated tools.

Life in Chaco Canyon was probably as pleasant as possible for the Stone Age. The residents had an elaborate naturalistic religion which entailed frequent and splendid community ceremonies. They engaged in trade which ranged as far as the Pacific Ocean and brought them, among other things, various shells and gems for jewelry. The Anasazi knew basket weaving before coming to Chaco and developed pottery after they settled in the Canyon. They wove cotton blankets and colored them with vegetable dyes. Some of their possessions were precious enough to them to be hidden in cleverly-concealed wall crypts which have been discovered only by chance.

The Anasazi left Chaco for unknown reasons, possibly drought, during the 13th century. Most residents moved east to the Pajarito Plateau, overlooking the Rio Grande Valley. The major settlement, among many, on the 8000-foot plateau was in Frijoles Canyon. The Canyon made an excellent homesite. Six miles long and a half mile wide, it is crossed by a small, spring-fed stream that carries ample water to irrigate the valley floor. Berries grow wild along the creek and tall pines, for lumber, cover the Canyon's southern slope. The sheer north wall is dotted with natural caves which some of the residents dug out and walled in for homes. Other residents lived in a circular communal structure, three stories high, near the creek.

The ruins of the Frijoles settlement are now a part of Bandelier National Monument, named for Adolph Bandelier, the first archaeologist to study the Pueblos. In a novel about the people of Frijoles Canyon, *The Delight Makers*, Bandelier speculated that they left the Canyon largely because of feuds and witchcraft within the community.

By the time the Spanish arrived in the area in 1540, most of the Pueblos had moved down from the Pajarito Plateau into the present villages along the Rio Grande Valley. Today there are 16 Pueblo communities in the Valley, in an area stretching about 75 miles both north and south of Santa Fe. The other three Pueblo villages in New Mexico, and the Hopi villages in Arizona, are west of the Valley.

The Spanish named the people of all of these towns "Pueblo," meaning community or village, because of their settled life. Actually each community, or pueblo, is a separate tribal group, with its own traditions and local laws. The people share a common cultural background and are still known generically as Pueblos, but they speak six different languages, varying considerably in some cases even among villages in close proximity.

In many respects life in the present pueblos is very similar to what the Spanish encountered over four centuries ago. The Spanish, and later the Americans, tried to introduce changes in Pueblo life, and did succeed to some degree, but on the whole ancient Pueblo traditions have prevailed. The extent of change varies substantially from one community to another, since each is fully independent and self-governing, but generally the Pueblos have accepted things they found useful and rejected anything that seemed likely to destroy the continuity of their way of life.

In government, the various villages have each retained the ancient form of council rule. The Spanish forced the Pueblos to choose a governor for each community, to act as a spokesman and liaison to the outside world, but important decisions are still made by a council of experienced leaders representing the most significant interests in the pueblo. In council, now as in the past, unanimity is the goal in reaching decisions, even when that requires interminable meetings or leaving an important matter unresolved for a considerable time. Religious leaders, *caciques*, are still influential in decisions, though they do not dominate councils as they did in the past.

Both the Spanish and the Americans attempted to eliminate the Pueblo religion. The Spanish were diligent in trying to convert the Indians to Catholicism — it was one of the primary reasons for their colonization of the area. Later the Americans arbitrarily assigned all Indians to various Christian churches and sent Protestant missionaries to the pueblos. One Baptist missionary was so zealous in his efforts at Laguna Pueblo that he caused a major split in the village which has never fully healed. The Spanish, who were usually more patient and persistent, were slightly more successful.

Most of the Pueblos accepted Catholicism to the degree that it did not interfere with their own ancient beliefs. Saints were easy to adopt because they were similar in some respects to the various Pueblo deities, usually called kachinas. Prayer and mass were sensible to the Pueblos, analogous to their own rituals, and the Christian calendar offered a few refinements over their own in tracking the important changes in the seasons. Other Christian concepts were more often tolerated than endorsed. The idea that sin requires a choice between damnation or redemption, one of the core beliefs of the religion, did not fit Pueblo social morality and does not figure prominently in their practice of Catholicism.

When the Pueblos adopted elements of Christianity, they regarded them as a supplement to their existing religion, not as a replacement. At first this was very frustrating to the Spanish, but they learned over time that efforts to suppress the old beliefs could be even more frustrating. The peaceful Pueblos killed overly-righteous priests, and in one instance organized the most effective mass routing that the Spanish empire ever encountered in the new world in response to an attempt to quash their religion. Eventually the two peoples reached a compromise. The Spanish began looking the other way and the Pueblos went underground — literally — with their religion. They banned the Spanish, and later the Americans, from their *kivas*, where they continued their most sacred ancient rites in seclusion. The villages which were distant from Spanish power, particularly Zuni and Hopi, stayed more open in their practices, which is why outsiders today are allowed to attend Zuni Shalako and to buy Hopi kachina dolls. The Rio Grande pueblos, in contrast, developed an intense secretiveness about their beliefs that has persisted to the present. Pueblo children are taught not to discuss the ancient religion with white people, and outsiders are prohibited from entering villages during sacred ceremonies when the masked kachinas appear.

In more ordinary and practical matters, the Pueblos have been less resistant to change. They have traded housing concepts freely, teaching the newcomers the use of adobe, while adopting Spanish building technologies and modern innovations as they have come along. Some Pueblos still live in large communal dwellings and reject electricity and piped water, like at Taos, but many others today live in houses which look depressingly suburban.

Livestock was an even easier adjustment. Cattle and sheep provided the same necessities as deer and buffalo and didn't have to be hunted. Besides, sheep supplied wool, which was simple to weave and much warmer than cotton.

The Pueblos quickly adopted Spanish weaving techniques and then passed them along to the Navajos. A Navajo legend claims that Spider Man and Spider Woman taught them to weave, but the evidence is clear that their real benefactors were their Pueblo enemies. The Pueblos used impermanent vegetable dyes on the wool, developed much earlier for their cotton cloth. The Navajos, however, experimented with durable and bright dyes introduced by the Spanish and soon surpassed their teachers in weaving skills. By the early 19th century the Spanish and Pueblos were acknowledging the proficiency of the Navajos and trading for their blankets. Some Pueblos continued to weave after that time, but they never made an effort to emulate the artistic and commercial success of their students.

The situation was different, though similar in some ways, in jewelry craftsmanship. The Pueblos mined turquoise in the Southwest, and made it into jewelry, before either the Spanish or the Navajos arrived in the region. Pueblo jewelers continued to work primarily with turquoise and other stones even after the Spanish introduced metalsmithing. At Santo Domingo they refined techniques for stringing turquoise and other materials into necklaces and earrings. Zuni jewelers use silver, but are known for their precise lapidary skills, employed in their traditional channel inlay and needlepoint styles. In these villages the Pueblos have maintained ancient jewelry skills in a widespread fashion and have achieved artistic and financial success with their work.

Again, though, as with weaving, the Navajos were more adaptable and commercially successful. They convinced the Spanish to teach them smithing about 1850, and began copying and modifying Spanish silver work. Navajo jewelers were making squash blossom necklaces and silver concha belts by the 1870s, using design ideas borrowed from Spanish silver bridles. In the next decade they discovered a technique for setting turquoise in silver, taking a precut stone and molding the metal to fit it.

Since these early days of Navajo smithing, for over 100 years, their silver work has been in high demand with traders and collectors. In recent decades one Pueblo group, the Hopi, have begun to produce some exceptional metal jewelry, but most Pueblo artisans are content in their own traditional attachment to turquoise.

In pottery the Pueblos have maintained a similar dedication to historical continuity. They still make pots by hand, as their ancestors did, without the use of a potter's wheel. Pueblo artists coil ropes of clay on top of one another to build up the walls of a piece, and then smooth the surface to eliminate any trace of the coils. The pots are fired outside in the open, instead of in a kiln, with dried dung cakes as the most common fuel.

Pottery has been the most refined Pueblo craft for hundreds of years and the only one that the Navajos haven't borrowed. There was a decline in craftsmanship about the turn of the century —after the railroad brought enamelware, tin pails, and other manufactured kitchen products to the area —but a significant renaissance began in the 1920s and has continued since.

Much of the stimulation for the renaissance came from the village of San Ildefonso, just north of Santa Fe. The most famous residents of the pueblo, Maria and Julian Martinez, developed a distinctive style of black pottery inspired by old fragments discovered in an archaeological dig. Maria was already an accomplished potter in 1919 when Julian worked out the technique for producing matte black designs on her polished black pots. The style was an immediate success, to such a degree that they began signing their work in 1925, which Pueblo artists had not done before.

The black-on-black style is still popular among San Ildefonso potters, but many of the best have created their own styles. Rose Gonzales introduced intaglio techniques at San Ildefonso in the 1930s, carving designs on the surface of the vessel. Later Blue Corn revived the polychromatic (multi-colored) style that had been common in the village in the 19th century. Her work influenced Popovi Da, Maria and Julian's son, to do some similar pots, even while he was assisting his mother at her work and developing a new firing technique of his own to make two-tone pieces of black and sienna. Popovi's son, Tony Da, often decorates his work with in-laid turquoise and heishi.

Some of these same styles and techniques are also found at Santa Clara, which is close to San Ildefonso in distance and in pottery reputation. Lela and Van Gutierrez developed a polychrome form at Santa Clara several decades ago that has been elaborated further by their children, Margaret and Luther. Sarafina and Geronimo Tafoya established a dynasty of potters which has produced work in a variety of modes, including the polished, carved ware that is most characteristic of Santa Clara. Their talented heirs include Margaret Tafoya, Camilio Tafoya, Christina Naranjo, Teresita Naranjo, Joseph Lonewolf, and Grace Medicine Flower.

At Hopi, Nampeyo inspired a dramatic resurgence of pottery in this century. Fascinated by sherds of ancient Hopi work, she developed the distinctive orange ware that became the dominant form in her village. Her daughters, granddaughters, and great-granddaughters, who normally use the Nampeyo name with their own in signing work, have perpetuated the tradition. In recent decades some Hopi artists have ventured into other styles, such as the white clay forms of Joy Navasie (Frogwoman) and Helen Naha (Featherwoman).

At Acoma, Lucy and Emma Lewis, Marie and Rose Chino, and other potters also use white clay, shaping it very thinly and decorating it with intricate geometric and animal designs or with more conventional polychrome patterns. The polychrome work at Zia, a well-established tradition in the pueblo, resembles some of the Acoma pottery, but is made with red clay.

A few villages, most notably Cochiti, tend to specialize in clay figurines instead of pots. In some ways these pieces reflect the curio orientation in Pueblo pottery that was popular before the current renaissance began, but many of them today are exquisite creations, particularly the storyteller figures of Helen Cordero and other talented Cochiti potters.

The artistry of these potters in the 20th century is the most visible sign today of Pueblo endurance and devotion to cultural heritage. The styles and design patterns of the pottery have been in flux, as they always have to some degree, but the substance of the craft has remained essentially the same for centuries. Pueblo artisans are still using basic elements of the original techniques developed by the Anasazi about 1500 years ago, and much of the inspiration for their current designs goes back to that earlier period.

Two of the most powerful nations of the modern world, imperial Spain and the United States, conquered the Pueblos during periods of vigorous expansion. They caused some changes in the way of life, but neither managed to complete the spiritual and cultural conquest that they intended. Pueblo pottery, religion, social customs, and other traditional practices remain a magnificent demonstration of the strength and vitality of a culture which developed long before either of the conquering nations.

Our Spanish forefathers

Our British forefathers came to the new world to escape from the old. They felt hopeless about their lives in England and wanted to carve a different destiny for themselves.

Our Spanish forefathers felt hopeless about almost nothing. They came to the new world to reshape it in the image of the old, on behalf of God, gold, and glory. Santa Fe was one of several miscalculations along the way. *La Villa Real de la Santa Fe de San Francisco*, the Royal City of the Holy Faith of St. Francis, did become an old world city, as the name implies, but it yielded little gold or glory and the native population took to God only in limited and frustrating ways.

Some of the first Spanish explorers to reach New Mexico might have guessed that fate in realistic moments, but hope affected the *Conquistadores* like blinders. Cabeza de Vaca, shipwrecked on the Texas coast in 1528, wandered the Southwest for eight years. His most impressive discovery was Indians living in permanent mud homes, growing corn, beans, and squash, but that was enough to inspire visions of cities of gold. A second small party, led by Friar Marcos de Niza, did not find the fabulous cities, but reported seeing them from a distant hilltop. The Friar's account stimulated the mounting of a major expedition, headed by Francisco Vasquez de Coronado, which included 300 volunteer soldiers, a band of Christian missionaries, and several hundred Mexican Indian servants. Coronado baptized some Indians in the Southwest between 1540 and 1542, but returned to Mexico City without glory or gold. His quest had cost about two million dollars in today's currency. Refusing to believe that the investment was futile, the authorities tried Coronado for not looking far enough.

The first colonizing expedition left Mexico City in 1598 with 130 families, hundreds of Indian servants, and "eight seraphic, apostolic, preaching priests," as they were described. They entered New Mexico, appropriately, with a flagellation rite, a fiesta, and a play. Arriving near the present site of El Paso on Holy Thursday, the colonists observed the day with medieval Penitente ceremonies that are still practiced in northern New Mexico. A chronicler among the colonists wrote that, "the soldiers, with cruel scourges, beat their backs unmercifully until the camp ran crimson with their blood. The humble Franciscan friars, barefoot and clothed in cruel thorny girdles, devoutly chanted their doleful hymns." Shortly afterwards, the group encountered some friendly Indians and celebrated possession of the new land. After a fiesta the colonists presented an edifying drama to the Indians, showing the natives joyfully welcoming the first priests and begging for baptism. The play may have been fun, but it wasn't much as prophecy.

The colonists settled originally at the San Juan Pueblo, north of Santa Fe, and immediately began the search for riches and souls. Typically, their reports were grander than their real discoveries. Within a few years the Franciscans claimed 60,000 Indian converts, probably three times the total native population of the area. One of them who traveled the region speculated on the local geography, reckoning that New Mexico was a peninsula extending northward between Newfoundland and China, within sight of the latter at some point yet to be found. The reports ran so contrary to actual experience that the main chronicler of the colony was later tried for writing "beautiful but untrue accounts."

Decimated by starvation, desertion, and

Indian revolts, the San Juan settlement was abandoned in 1610 in favor of a new beginning at Santa Fe. Life remained fragile and rough for the colonists in the new location, but they gradually began to adjust their expectations and adapt to the environment. They survived a meager existence for several generations before famine and religious passion created a major disturbance.

In the 1670s a drought forced colonists and Indians into subsisting on hides boiled with roots and herbs, which probably caused the epidemic that followed. In the midst of this distress, the Spanish governor decided to obliterate all traces of Pueblo religion. Many of the natives had accepted Catholicism, but only as a supplement to their traditional beliefs, which they never considered dropping. The governor tried 47 Pueblo shamans for sorcery and hanged three. For his own good he should have executed at least four, because one of those released, Pope, was a charismatic and powerful leader. Pope devised a masterful plan for a mass insurrection against the Spanish and organized the various pueblos to carry it out simultaneously. On August 10, 1680, the Indians began slaughtering the Spanish, starting with outlying villages and moving toward Santa Fe. Spanish survivors barricaded themselves in the Palace of the Governors as the Indians burned the town around them. Eventually the Pueblos, who have never enjoyed war, allowed the survivors to flee south to El Paso.

The Spanish colonists remained there for 12 years, until new recruits could be mustered for a reconquest. To lead the return, the Viceroy of New Spain chose Don Diego de Vargas, a proven soldier from an illustrious Madrid family. De Vargas' initial expedition to Santa Fe in 1692 encountered no resistance, and he went back to Mexico proclaiming a peaceful reconquest. When De Vargas returned the following year, however, to re-establish the colony, the Indians fought back.

He had to take the Palace of the Governors by force and afterwards executed 70 of the defenders and enslaved 400 others. The Pueblos continued to resist the Spanish for three bloody years before the reconquest was completed.

The colonists had to rebuild Santa Fe totally. The Palace of the Governors was intact, and the walls of the San Miguel Mission were still standing, but the Indians had razed everything else. As before, the colonists built in adobe, using construction concepts borrowed from the Pueblos. Adobe bricks, containing mud and straw, were formed and sun-dried at the building site. They were laid together with wet adobe and later plastered with the same mixture to make walls that were too thick to be pierced by arrows. Houses were built close to the ground, with low ceilings and flat roofs, never over one story until the late 19th century. The roof was supported by pine logs, or *vigas*, laid on top of the walls. The home of an *hidalgo* differed from that of a peasant primarily in the length of the *vigas*, which determined the size of the rooms. On top of the *vigas* were small slats of wood and then brush and earth, graded to drain water. The floors were dirt, mixed with animal blood to pack them. In most rooms there was a small corner fireplace, made to take upright logs.

The furnishings in homes were simple and crude in the colonial period. Even *hidalgos* had little furniture beyond hand-hewn chests, benches, stools, and a table. Generally these articles were made locally, since Santa Fe's isolation precluded the importation of many bulky objects.

The religious art which decorated homes and churches was easier to bring from Spain and Mexico, though much of it was made locally, too. *Retablos*, religious paintings on flat boards, were almost always imported until the 19th century because drawing skills and paints were rare in the early colony. Woodcarving skills were more common, used in the decoration of *vigas* and furniture, and in making *bultos*, wooden statues. Most of the *bultos* were images of saints, called *santos*, though carvers also made *reredos*, or altar screens, and *muertes*, the distinctive death carts that are a vivid symbol of the colonists' familiarity with the end of life.

Doctors were scarce in the colony. For awhile in the 18th century, there was one "surgeon and dentist" in town whose equipment seemed to impress residents more than his success rate. He had "two cases for instruments, one with five razors, and whetstone, and the other one with six lancets trimmed with tortoise shell and silver." During most of the colonial period, residents relied on home remedies, using herbs, other plants, and whiskey distilled in the area.

In the homes of *los ricos*, the rich, these medical staples were kept in carefully-controlled storerooms, along with hanging meat cuts and strings of dried fruit and chile. Wealth was based on the amount of land and sheep owned, but everyone was a farmer. In the summer there was fresh corn, beans, onions, and various fruits, but for most of the year the colonists ate dried produce and corn meal made into tortillas. Meals were cooked in the fireplace in heavy kettles, or outside in *hornos*, beehive-shaped adobe ovens, and were served generally on pottery, much of it made by the Pueblos.

When working at home, women wore full, short skirts of serge and tight, low-necked blouses that some early American visitors considered indecent. When they left the house, women who could afford it wrapped themselves in imported shawls, or, for special occasions, dressed in European finery. They often used red clay for rouge, but switched to a heavy white powder of ground bones for *fandangos,* or dances.

Men often had a more extensive and expensive wardrobe than women, because of their exclusive hold on official and ceremonial roles in the colony. *Hidalgos* needed fancy uniforms, with gold lace if possible, for military formalities. At other times they wore woolen pantaloons, leather jackets, and high boots, well suited for riding. Wool *serapes* and imported flat *sombreros* protected them from the weather.

Fabrics used in most clothes were woven locally. The most common cloth was *sabanilla,* a woolen plain-weave made in large quantities for basic garments and bedding. It was sometimes embroidered with floral or geometric designs in the distinctive long *colcha* stitch.

In the latter colonial period weaving became a refined craft in New Mexico. At the same time that the Navajos were developing their weaving skills, the Spanish were independently establishing a similar tradition, known as Rio Grande weaving. Both the Spanish and the Navajos were influenced heavily by design patterns which originated in the Orient and were transmitted to them primarily through Saltillo weavings from Mexico. Rio Grande blankets and rugs are not as well known today as their Navajo counterparts, but Spanish artisans did some exceptional work.

Life was austere in the colony on the whole, crafted by hand from scarce resources. But it did not lack gaiety. Fiestas in celebration of Mardi Gras, Easter, Christmas, saints' days, marriages, and other special occasions were frequent and important. When Mexico won its independence from Spain in 1821, the festivities in Santa Fe went on for five days. On the first morning the residents raised the new flag and then joined in a spontaneous parade. Afterwards, everyone gathered at the Palace. The head of the city council led a cotillion, which opened a grand *baile,* or ball, where celebrants danced to lively guitar and violin versions of the same tunes that were played more solemnly in church. A puritanical American trader who happened to be in town was shocked at the revelry. "All classes abandoned themselves to the most reckless dissipation," including "vice and licentiousness of every description," which went on "night and day" with "no time for sleep."

A generation later, when the U.S. Army seized Santa Fe from Mexico, there were no celebrations. Suddenly New Mexico was severed from its historical and cultural roots in the Spanish colonial empire. The residents gradually adjusted to the new situation, after a few ineffective attempts at insurrection, but for many years afterwards there were more army band concerts than fiestas on the plaza.

Fortunately, the Spanish heritage was too strong to perish, despite the attempts of some early Americans to destroy it. Most of the native population still knows and uses the Spanish language, though they have also mastered English and can now avoid the property swindles perpetrated on their grandparents. The U.S. Army suppressed the annual fiesta in honor of Don Diego de Vargas and his feats of the 1690s, but the fiesta was revived later and Don Diego is once again celebrated as a legendary hero, more important locally than George Washington. Spanish Catholic traditions, so different from those of the conquering soldiers, have persisted, from delightful Christmas customs to Penitente flagellations at Easter.

The strength of the Spanish heritage today is particularly evident in the vitality of colonial crafts. Weaving and woodcarving died out in Santa Fe in the late 19th century, but the local traditions were maintained and refined in small mountain villages north of the city. The recent work of weavers like Juanita Jaramillo, Maria

Vergara-Wilson, John Trujillo, and the Ortega and Cordova families, reflects a commitment to preserve and extend the Rio Grande style. Luis Tapia, Leo Salazar, Horacio Valdez, Frederico Vigil, Ben Ortega, and several members of the Lopez family have all carved *santos* as reverent and expressive as any made locally in the 18th and 19th centuries. Other carvers, inspired by Felipe Archuleta, have taken local traditions in new directions, creating wonderful wooden sculptures of watermelons and animals.

As long as these artisans and other area residents remain proud of their heritage, Santa Fe will continue to be predominantly Spanish. Their ancestors didn't find gold, or fully convert many Indians, but they did entrench their way of life in an area very remote from home. Although Santa Fe has changed considerably since the days of the original colonists, it is still the outpost of the old world in the new that they wanted to establish.

The army and the art colony

In Santa Fe the term "Anglo" has very broad application. Used for almost anyone who is not Hispanic or Indian, it is a polite way of saying non-native, or outsider, in contrast with the more pejorative term "gringo." It has been applied, at times at least, to Italians, Jews, Blacks, and even an occasional Briton.

The first Anglos to visit Santa Fe were escorted into town under military guard, as prisoners, just a few years before the city's 200th anniversary. A small party of U.S. explorers trespassed on the Spanish empire accidentally in the winter of 1805-06. Under orders from President Thomas Jefferson to find the sources of western tributaries of the Mississippi River, Lieutenant Zebulon Pike and his men stumbled instead upon the headwaters of the Rio Grande in the Colorado Rockies. A Spanish militia unit arrested the Americans and took them to Santa Fe for questioning, treating them more as curiosities than as captives.

Local policy toward Anglo visitors changed considerably in the following two decades. When Mexico won its independence from Spain, the new republic wanted to establish good relations with its republican neighbors to the northeast. In 1821 a Mexican militia unit from Santa Fe encountered a group of Missourians, wandering the plains trading with Indians. The Santa Feans invited the traders to return home with them to sell their wares, opening the Santa Fe Trail.

Thousands of Anglos came and went over the Trail between Missouri and Santa Fe in the next half century. At its peak of activity trade along the Trail employed 10,000 men and grossed millions of dollars annually for both Mexican and American merchants.

The existence of the Trail made Santa Fe a natural target for the United States in the 1846-48 war with Mexico. President James K. Polk started the war mainly to acquire California from Mexico, to realize America's "manifest destiny" of expanding to the Pacific Ocean. Santa Fe was occupied on the way to California.

The U.S. Army stayed for the rest of the 19th century and became an important presence in the city. The soldiers' impressions were not very favorable. One of them wrote home about his "perfect contempt" for the city and another called it "the Siberia of America." Santa Fe was to them, as a third soldier described it, "a dirty, filthy place built entirely of mud." The Army erected a sawmill as soon as it arrived, with the intention of replacing adobe buildings with proper wood structures.

This feeling about adobe prevailed among Anglo residents until the early 20th century. There was still a good deal of adobe construction in Santa Fe in the territorial period, before New Mexico gained statehood in 1912, but almost everyone who could afford it wanted to use milled lumber and brick for trim at least. Many of the historic homes of the city were modified during this period in the territorial style, most noticeably with decorative layers of brick along roof lines and Greek Revival doors, windows, and portals. The ideal for most Anglo residents was an all brick house with a pitched roof, like those in their Eastern home towns.

Attitudes changed along with Anglo settlement patterns about the time that statehood was granted. With New Mexico firmly incorporated into the United States, and the Navajos and Apaches of the area conquered, the U.S. Army moved out. As the soldiers left, anthropologists and artists moved in.

The anthropologists were attracted initially by the work of Adolph Bandelier, a Swiss scholar of international reputation who lived in Santa Fe in the 1880s. Bandelier's studies of the Pueblos stimulated considerable interest in North American prehistory. In 1907 the Archaeological Institute of America opened a center in Santa Fe, the School of American Research. The early leaders of the School, particularly Edgar Hewett and Sylvanus Morley, replaced the army colonels as the prime molders of Anglo opinion in the city. Unlike their predecessors, the anthropologists understood and appreciated the historical character of Santa Fe and wanted it preserved. They helped to inspire a revival of the Spanish Pueblo architectural style which still influences most new construction in the city.

Painters and writers of the early Santa Fe art colony assisted energetically in the preservation efforts. They began arriving in Santa Fe about a decade after the anthropologists but soon had the scholars outnumbered. By the 1920s the art colony was a major factor in Santa Fe life and since then it has been the primary Anglo influence in the city.

The first Anglo artists in the area settled in Taos in the 1890s. Ernest Blumenschein was a popular and successful artist in the East when he passed through Taos doing illustrations for a magazine article. He and his friend Bert Phillips, another established artist, were eager to escape the hectic, urban pace of the art centers of the East. Attracted immediately to the serenity and primitive charm of New Mexico, they moved permanently to Taos in the last years of the 19th century.

Blumenschein and Phillips, along with several other recognized artists who followed them west, formed the Taos Society of Artists in 1912. Generally educated in Paris, the Society members were highly talented within the representational traditions of their day. Their literal documentation of New Mexico life was so popular elsewhere that the Santa Fe Railroad commissioned paintings by Society members to hang in their offices and put on calendars, as advertising in the early days of the tourism business.

The Santa Fe art colony began forming in the early 1910s. The leading figures of the first decade were Robert Henri and John Sloan, both of whom continued to live mainly in New York, though Sloan maintained a summer home in Santa Fe for over 30 years. A number of less-established artists moved to the city permanently in the same period. Five of these artists, all under thirty and newly arrived in town, banded together for a show at the Museum of Fine Arts in 1921, calling themselves *Los Cinco Pintores*, the five painters. A spirited group, influenced by Cezanne and Post-Impressionism, they reacted against the prestige of the Taos Society and declared that their purpose was "to take art to the people and not surrender to commercialism." The work of Jozef Bakos, Fremont Ellis, Walter Mruk, Willard Nash, and Will Shuster seems quite traditional today, but that was not the intent or the public reaction originally. The same was true of other contemporaries of *Los Cincos Pintores* in Santa Fe, such as B.J.O. Nordfeldt and Gustave Baumann.

In the 1920s the international avant-garde invaded New Mexico. Mable Dodge Luhan, once described as "a reposeful hurricane," moved her radical salon from New York City to Taos during the conservative backlash following World War I. She "willed," as she put it, an international roster of visitors, including D.H. Lawrence, Max Weber, Paul and Rebecca Strand (who brought Georgia O'Keeffe with them), John Marin, Marsden Hartley, and Andrew Dasburg. Edmund Wilson described the resident circle in 1930 as an "extraordinary population of rich people, writers, and artists who pose as Indians, cowboys, prospectors, desperadoes, Mexicans and other nearly extinct species." Two of Luhan's guests — O'Keeffe and Dasburg — stayed in the area and became legendary presences.

During the Depression and into the 1950s, the art colony of Santa Fe grew as slowly as the rest of the city. A few major artists, such as Laura Gilpin, Eliot Porter, and Agnes Martin, moved to the area in this period, but the next large influx of Anglo artists began in the 1960s. Paul Sarkisian and Fritz Scholder started an immigration from California that later included Larry Bell, Ken Price, and Bruce Nauman. In 1970 Clinton Adams moved the Tamarind Institute from Los Angeles to Albuquerque, stimulating a significant upsurge in printmaking in New Mexico and establishing Albuquerque as another center for artists in the state.

Most of the new arrivals in the last couple of decades have been young artists, coming to the area without established reputations. Many of them have made distinctive use of the local environment, cultural and natural, in their work. The irony and pop imagery that Scholder applied to Indian subject matter in the 1960s became characteristic of much of the best work of the area in the 1970s. Luis Jimenez developed sophisticated fiberglass sculptures of cowboy and Indian scenes which reflect the popular mythology of the West in glittery plastic. John Fincher makes skilled and sharp-edged paintings about such regional symbols as cacti, knives, boots, and spurs. Ken Saville's drawings and constructions place human frailty and darkness in the vibrant context of colorful Southwestern images. John Wenger, Carl Johansen, Richard Thompson, Reg Loving, John Rise, Tom Palmore, and others are also doing striking work in a similar vein.

Other contemporary area artists work in more familiar styles, both abstract and representational. Among the abstract painters who have received some national recognition are Jean Promutico, Gene Newmann, Susan Rowland, Allan Graham, Zach Rieke, Frank Ettenberg, Janell Wicht, Margaret Newman, and Helen Beck. Ford Ruthling, Doug West, Forrest Moses, Eli Levin, Bruce Lowney, Jim Wood, Doug Atwill, Dick Mason, Wilson Hurley, Clark Hulings, Tom Berg, Douglas Johnson, Bill Shepherd, Dennis Culver, Laurence Sisson, Geoffrey Landis, and Woody Gwyn use figurative elements in their work to varying degrees. Photographers of the area, including Paul Caponigro, Danny Lyon, Elliot McDowell, and Meridel Rubenstein, employ documentary techniques primarily.

Working alongside these Anglo artists today are a number of significant Indian painters and sculptors. Apache Allan Houser sculpts graceful, fluid figures while his son, Bob Haozous, uses pop imagery. Painters and printmakers such as Helen Hardin, Dan Namingha, Kevin RedStar, John Nieto, Armand Lara, Ed Singer, and the late T.C. Cannon are both representational and allegorical in their work. R.C. Gorman, a Navajo living in Taos, has been very successful with his minimalist drawings of Indian women. Jaune Quick-to-See Smith and Randy Lee White are young artists with tremendous promise whose work is at once traditional in its tribal references and elements of style, but also very contemporary in concept and resonance.

Sculpture around Santa Fe is centered at the Shidoni Foundry and Gallery in Tesuque. Every summer for its annual show, Shidoni fills 8 1/2 acres with sculpture, much of it created in the area. The work ranges from the Western bronzes of Lloyd Woodbury to the large, abstract pieces of owner T.C. Hicks. The work of Charles Pebworth, David Anderson, Una Hanbury, Ed

Vega, Jesus Bautista Moroles, and other area sculptors is also shown in a few other local galleries.

Much of the current ceramic work being done in New Mexico could be classified as sculpture instead of pottery. The clay constructions of Gloria Graham, Rick Dillingham, Juan Hamilton, Bev Maghennis, and Timothy Moore have no function beyond their form.

Functional or not, ceramics and other crafts are a vital part of the art colony today. There were very few Anglo crafts artists in the early years of the colony, but their numbers have swelled incredibly since the 1960s. The areas of greatest concentration — ceramics, woodwork, weaving, and jewelry — are the same ones in which the indigenous traditions of the area are strongest. The dramatic increase in the number of local Anglo artisans in recent decades, added to the native Indian and Spanish artisans, gives New Mexico an easy lead over other states in the quantity and quality of crafts work.

The diversity of media and style makes the art colony today less cohesive than in the past, and less focused in its local influence, but its impact on Santa Fe is more pervasive than ever. The adobe-hating soldiers of the U.S. Army might have found another way to California if they had known the future they were opening. Certainly Ernest Blumenschein would be startled by what he began. He would understand, no doubt, why the Anglo art colony has continued to flourish, but would be amused, at best, to learn that it is as full of galleries and collectors as the fast-paced art centers of the East that he left so far behind in the 1890s.

Part Two

The living museum

A plaza walk

Ten years before the Pilgrims landed at Plymouth Rock, some 50 Spanish soldiers and their families were erecting crude mud and timber shelters around the central plaza of Santa Fe. The original plaza was larger than it is today, extending east in a rectangular shape to the site of the present Cathedral. In the 17th century, while the Puritans were settling the rest of New England, mounted soldiers in medieval armor used the plaza as an assembly and drill ground. Anything of a public nature — proclamations, games, markets, fiestas — occurred there as well. Since those early years, for almost four centuries, the plaza has been the center of Santa Fe life.

In later periods the plaza housed a bull ring, an elaborate bandstand for concerts by the Ft. Marcy Army Band, and now an uninspired obelisk. It's where Mexican independence from Spain was celebrated in 1821 and where General Kearney proclaimed the annexation of New Mexico by the United States to an unenthusiastic citizenry in 1846. Today the plaza is the site of Indian Market, Spanish Market, and much of Fiesta, annual occasions when it still tolerates hordes of happy traders and rowdy celebrants.

Its most tumultuous period was in the mid-19th century, when it was the end of the Santa Fe Trail. As the Yankee traders approached Santa Fe at the end of their 70-day journey from Missouri, they whipped up their teams and charged the plaza, shouting and cracking 12-foot whips, scattering dust, dogs, and chickens in all directions. Before slowing down, the long wagon trains, carrying about 5,000 pounds of merchandise each, raced in a great spiral about the four sides of the plaza. Crowds gathered quickly, eager for outside news, new provisions, and the chance to make some money from the high-living, road-weary visitors. As the plaza filled with wagons, the traders made their way around the gambling rooms that lined nearby streets, playing *monte* and dancing *fandangos* with the "relentlessly coquettish *mujeres* of Santa Fe," as one trader described the ladies.

Facing north from the plaza, towards the Palace of the Governors, one might be able to imagine another raucous moment, fortunately briefer, in the past. In 1680 there were 2,500 Pueblo Indians looking angrily in the same direction, chanting songs of vengeance day and night, determined to drive the Spanish from their land. Barricaded in the Palace, which was larger then, were 1,000 terrified people and many more starving sheep, mules, horses, goats, and cattle. The Indians had already killed several hundred Spaniards in villages north of Santa Fe and were now plundering and burning the church at the east end of the plaza. One of the Pueblo leaders, wrapped in red taffeta taken from the church, offered the Spanish a choice of two crosses, one red for war and the other white for a peaceful departure. The Spanish elected to stay and fight, but they didn't have a chance. The water supply for the Palace crossed by the plaza in an irrigation ditch. The Indians easily diverted the *acequia* and expelled the Spanish for over 12 years. The peaceful Pueblos forced the Spanish empire into a more serious retreat than the mighty Aztec and Incan warriors ever managed.

Browsing along the way

The Pueblos returned the Palace and the plaza to the Spanish in the 1690s, but this is not very evident in scanning the area today. The Pueblos have come back in force in recent years, bearing pots and bracelets this time instead of fire. Only Indian artisans are allowed to sell work

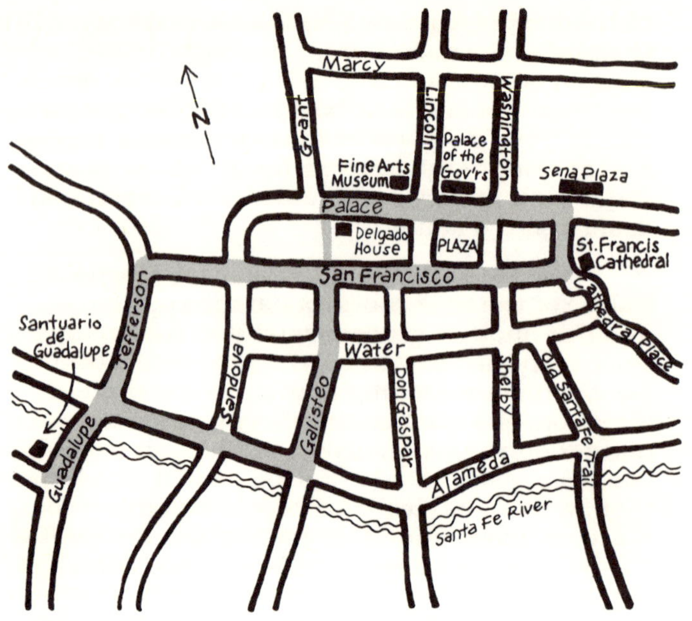

under the portal of the Palace and they are there almost every day, stoically accepting the stares and questions of curious visitors along with their money.

On the other three sides of the plaza, and along nearby streets, are some of the best Indian art and crafts galleries in town. The Dewey-Kofron Gallery, the Kiva, and Packard's, all directly on the plaza, provide a good introduction to the range and quality of contemporary Indian work. A little south on Old Santa Fe Trail are several galleries, including The Gallery Wall and Santa Fe East. W.S. Dutton's Rare Things is two blocks east on Palace Avenue, and Indian Trader West and Cristof's are a couple of blocks west on San Francisco Street.

The Palace of the Governors

The Palace is the oldest government building

in the United States, in continuous use since 1610. Over one hundred rulers — Spanish, Pueblo, Mexican, and American — have occupied the building. From this spot some of them claimed sovereignty over half of the present-day United States, east to the Mississippi River, west to the Pacific Ocean, and south into the Mexican state of Chihuahua.

The original structure built by the first Spanish governor, Pedro de Peralta, extended much farther north and west than the present Palace. The enclosed central patio was large enough for a ten-acre vegetable garden. There was no portal then, but there were defense towers on the two corners of the front facing the plaza.

When the Indians evicted the Spanish in 1680, they transformed the Palace into a typical Pueblo village. The small Spanish windows and doors were blocked up and rooms were entered from the top by ladders. The structure, like the Taos Pueblo, grew upwards, probably to three or four stories. One of the towers was converted into a *kiva*, which the returning Spanish reluctantly used for their own worship for over a decade, until they completed a new parish church.

Almost everything except the roof beams, or *vigas*, was originally made of dirt. The walls, then as now, were adobe. The dirt floor was mixed with animal blood to pack it and produce a sheen. It wasn't until the late 19th century that tin replaced the dirt roof piled several feet high above the *vigas*. One 19th century resident of Santa Fe called it the "roof garden." "Most every desert plant grew and flowered and died a natural death in the five feet of earth which held the moisture of ordinary downpours but let the cloudbursts trickle through. The inside was really the only place where we had any need for umbrellas; outside the continuous line of portals protected us." The place has seldom, if ever, looked like a palace.

Probably the best known today of the Palace's many residents was U.S. Territorial Governor Lew Wallace, author of *Ben Hur,* who lived there in the 1880s. Wallace's description of his writing chamber would probably have applied to many rooms in the Palace at the time. "The walls were grimy, the undressed boards of the floor rested flat upon the ground; the cedar rafters, rain-stained as those in the dining-hall of Cedric the Saxon, and overweighted by tons and tons of mud composing the roof, had the threatening downward curvature of a shipmate's cutlass."

The building has always been relatively expensive to maintain because of its construction and size. Spanish, Mexican, and U.S. governors were constantly petitioning their various central governments for money for repairs, but never got as much as they requested. The upkeep costs made the Palace a political football at the turn of the century. The U.S. Government granted the building, and its maintenance costs, to the territorial government of New Mexico. The governor protested, saying the territory couldn't afford it. He offered it to the Smithsonian Institution, which rejected it as an unmanageable property. Stuck with possession, the legislature decided in 1909 to make the Palace into the Museum of New Mexico and appropriated funds for its restoration.

At first the Palace housed all of the Museum of New Mexico. Since then separate facilities have been built in Santa Fe for the Museum's collection of art (Museum of Fine Arts), folk art (Museum of International Folk Art), and anthropology (Laboratory of Anthropology). The Museum uses the Palace today for historical exhibitions.

The Museum of Fine Arts

The Museum of Fine Arts, directly west of the Palace, had a unique beginning among American art museums. Most museums originate as repositories for life-long collections of art patrons. When the Museum of Fine Arts opened in 1917, it was the first in the United States and one of the few since then, inspired by local artists for exhibits of their current work.

As soon as the Museum of New Mexico was established in the Palace of the Governors, the first director, Dr. Edgar Hewett, began thinking about a separate art museum. At first he set up a small gallery within the Palace and provided free studios to artists in the back of the building. Predictably, demands on this space grew, and within a few years Hewett managed to convince the legislature to build an art museum across the street from the Palace.

Robert Henri and John Sloan, established artists from the East who spent a good deal of time in Santa Fe, were Hewett's advisers on policy for the new museum. They advocated the "open-door" approach that the Museum took for many years, allowing any local artist to exhibit new work on a first-come, first-served basis. No effort was made to acquire a collection of Old Masters from past centuries and distant places, though gradually the Museum did begin building a collection of New Mexico artists. After a few decades the collection was substantial and included some important works by the earliest artists in the area, who were becoming known by then as Old Masters themselves. As the collection became more valuable, art patrons of the city became more active in the affairs of the Museum and the artists were dispossessed of their role. The quality of exhibitions has been more consistent since the elimination of the open-door policy, but some of the Museum's vitality was also sacrificed.

The Museum was built on land once occupied by the western part of the Palace of the

Governors and later, in the 19th century, by U.S. Army barracks. The structure was an early and influential expression of the modern Spanish Pueblo architectural style. Completed in 1917, the building fused traditional designs and materials with elements of modern efficiency and comfort. Its massive walls, terraces, and recessions reflect the organic lines of Pueblo buildings. The Spanish Franciscan mission churches, particularly the one at Acoma, inspired the St. Francis Auditorium, on the west end of the building, an entrancing spot for the concerts and other performances held there. On its completion residents and visitors alike hailed the synthesis of traditions represented in the new building and it became a model for the style that still guides architectural design in the city.

Delgado House (124 West Palace Avenue)

In 1776 Manuel Delgado enlisted in the Royal Army of Spain and was assigned duty in Santa Fe. The family rose in prominence over the years and shifted its ambitions from military glory to the more lucrative trade of the Santa Fe Trail. By the third generation, Captain Delgado's grandchildren were being sent to school in St. Louis and were learning young the ways of the Trail from their student travel. One of the grandchildren, Felipe B. Delgado, became one of the principal owners of the wagon trains that crossed the plains and operated a large general store in Santa Fe.

In 1970 architect John Gaw Meem purchased the house from the Delgado family, restored it, and gave it to the Historic Santa Fe Foundation. Meem had come to Santa Fe in the 1920s to recover from tuberculosis and stayed to become the leading designer of the Spanish Pueblo architectural style. His integrity, taste, and persistence were major factors in the appearance of Santa Fe today.

Browsing along the way

Nearby on Palace Avenue are two major galleries where one can compare the styles of the early and recent years of the local art colony. Steve O'Meara, whose gallery is on the same side of the street as the Delgado House, handles work of the Founders. Elaine Horwitch, across the street, represents some of the most exciting contemporary artists of the area.

Between O'Meara's Gallery and the Palace Restaurant, there is a passageway south to San Francisco Street, which returns to the plaza. A short, worthwhile detour leads to the Santuario de Nuestra Senora de Guadalupe, two blocks west on San Francisco and one block south on Guadalupe Street.

Santuario de Nuestra Senora de Guadalupe

Built in the last few years of the 18th century, the Chapel of Our Lady of Guadalupe was designed and constructed in the style typical of New Mexico church architecture of that period. The walls, floor, and roof were adobe, and the shape was cruciform. The three-tiered tower contained sand-cast copper bells.

When a new, larger church was built on the property in 1961, the Chapel was no longer used for mass. After several years of neglect, the parishioners restored it in its original style. The attention to detail in the restoration is seen in the red altar wall. Ox blood was added to the plaster to reproduce the 18th century appearance.

Browsing along the way

The best way to return to San Francisco Street is to go east on Alameda to Galisteo Street. Along Galisteo are several locally-popular shops. When residents want Hispanic crafts work to complement the style of local homes, they usually try Artesanos and the Old Mexico Shop, both of which carry fine imports. If they are looking instead for Spanish folk cures or unusual seasonings, they would likely try Lujan's Place, an old-style herb and kitchen shop.

San Francisco Street

Named for St. Francis, the patron saint of Santa Fe, San Francisco Street was established in its current course by the mid-18th century. The earliest extant map of the city, done in the 1760s, shows the intersection of San Francisco and Galisteo. "Camino de Galisteo" on the map cuts through fields from the south and has very few buildings on it. To the right at the intersection were adobe buildings, mainly long and narrow, lining San Francisco Street down to the parish church where the Cathedral now stands. To the left was a small residence, more fields, and then the large *hacienda* of Nicholas Ortiz III.

Nicholas III was the grandson of a colonist who came to Santa Fe in 1693, at the time of the Spanish reconquest. Serving as a captain in the royal army when the map was drawn, Nicholas III would soon be killed by Comanches. His son, Antonio Jose Ortiz, inherited the *hacienda* and made it even larger after he became a successful trader and rancher.

Just north across San Francisco Street from the Ortiz house and the Galisteo intersection was the rowdy gambling district of Santa Fe in the 19th century. It was here that buffalo hunters, *vaqueros*, politicians, traders, and soldiers came to drink the raw whiskey called Taos Lightning, to play *monte*, and to find love or a semblance of it with lavender-powdered *senoritas* in black veils. The strongest personality of them all was the beautiful and shrewd Dona Tules Barcelo, who owned the largest and fanciest of the gambling halls, and a bank as well. One puritanical trader, who referred to the *cantinas* as "pandemoniums," called Dona Tules a woman "of very loose habits," and was shocked that she was "openly received in the first circles of society." He imagined with pleasure how she would have been rejected socially in Eastern cities, but felt exasperated that she wouldn't have cared. Ruth Laughlin has told Dona Tules' story in fictional form in *The Wind Leaves No Shadows.*

Browsing along the way

Along San Francisco and intersecting streets, going east towards the Cathedral, are a number of galleries and shops, with new ones being added constantly at the time of publication. The Contemporary Craftsman (on Don Gaspar) carries a broad and interesting selection of local crafts, and The Gamut (on San Francisco) mixes some fine Southwestern work with a range of imports. Other crafts galleries in the area, such as Arius Tile (next to the Contemporary Craftsman), the Santa Fe Weaving Center (on Galisteo), and Arachne Fiberarts (on San Francisco), specialize in one medium.

San Francisco Street is also popular for clothes shopping. La Mariquita imports beautiful, festive Hispanic dresses, and Origins imports less traditional women's wear that is more common on Santa Fe streets today. Morningbird and Suzette's appeal to young women with more classic interests. Salamander Leathers has two shops on San Francisco—the smaller one for men—which feature a variety of fine leather goods, and Overland Sheepskin (on Galisteo) carries a range of warm wool and leather products made in Taos.

On and near the plaza are some important art galleries. Marilyn Butler represents fine contemporary painters of the area and Los Llanos combines similar work with books. The Jamison Gallery and Woodrow Wilson Fine Arts handle representational work. West from the plaza on San Francisco are several galleries which specialize in different fields, including the Santa Fe Gallery of Photography, The White Hyacinth (art posters), and the Culpepper Gallery (Spanish colonial paintings).

Cathedral of St. Francis

The Cathedral is the most visible legacy of the most influential person in local history, Bishop Jean Baptiste Lamy, whose bronze statue stands in front of the Cathedral. It is ironic that a Frenchman played such a major role in shaping the fortunes of a Spanish colonial town in the American West. The irony is reflected well in the contrast between the Romanesque style of the Cathedral and the rest of local architecture.

Willa Cather has gracefully described Lamy's life in Santa Fe (as Bishop Latour) in *Death Comes for the Archbishop.* Arriving in 1851 during a wild frontier period in the village, when the Church's authority was disintegrating throughout the Southwest, Lamy energetically restored clerical influence, established schools and a hospital, and gradually instilled a sense of refinement into Santa Fe life. It was unfortunate that his own notion of refinement always remained European, not fully sympathetic to local ways. His tastes, and his predeliction for modern progress, had some adverse effects on the town, but he served well and was much loved.

Bishop Lamy wanted a cathedral in Santa Fe that expressed God's glory with the same magnificence as the churches in his native Auvergne. The parish church, or *parroquia,* which he used as his cathedral for many years was a simple adobe structure started in 1714. Lamy and his French architects built the new cathedral around the old *parroquia,* making it much wider and half again as long, but retaining and using the old church until the new one was completed. The cornerstone, elaborately engraved for the occasion, was laid with high ceremony in 1869 and promptly stolen. Construction proceeded anyway, using stone from nearby quarries and Italian stone cutters, and continued until 1886, the year after the Bishop's retirement. The original French plans, which were never carried out fully, called for steeples rising 160 feet from the two towers.

The most interesting part of St. Francis Cathedral is what is left of the old *parroquia*, the Chapel of Our Lady of the Rosary. The choir loft of the Chapel and part of its walls were removed in constructing the new church, making it smaller than before, but it has been in continuous use since 1718. The Chapel is dedicated to the oldest madonna in North America, a small 16th century wooden statue carved in Mexico and brought to Santa Fe about 1625. She was originally known as Our Lady of the Assumption, but was renamed *La Conquistadora* (Our Lady of the Conquest) after she accompanied the Spanish in exile from 1680 to 1693 and returned with them as a protector during the reconquest from the Indians. The Chapel was built in her honor on the site of the original parish church, which was destroyed by the Pueblos in 1680. Though her association with these passions of old has faded somewhat, *La Conquistadora* has remained the community's most important symbol of Spanish unity and religious devotion.

Sena Plaza

Another of the heroes of the Spanish reconquest was Captain Arias de Quiros. His feats lag a reverential distance behind *La Conquistadora's* in the community's memory, but in his day he got the more tangible reward of a large land grant directly north of the Cathedral site.

The captain's land grant included all of the

area now covered by the long, low portal that runs down Palace Avenue to Washington Street, and considerably more. Arias de Quiros cultivated most of the land and lived in a two-room house, nothing of which remains.

The courtyard of Sena Plaza, which can be entered directly across from Cathedral Place, was the scene of grand Spanish hospitality in the late 19th century, hosted by Dona Isabel and Don Jose Sena. From a small house he inherited on the property, Don Jose gradually built a *hacienda* of 33 rooms. He and Dona Isabel and their eleven children occupied the south, east, and west sides of the courtyard. Horses, chickens, and servants were quartered along the north front. Their home was one story except on the west side, where outside stairways led up to a large ballroom, a room sufficient in size to hold the legislative assembly temporarily when the capitol burned in 1892. The second stories on the eastern and northern portions of the building were added in the 1920s during a dedicated and expert restoration.

There are two smaller courtyards along this block of Palace, on the way back to the central plaza. L. Bradford Prince owned the *hacienda* and patio that now serve The Shed Restaurant at 113 East Palace. The Manhattan Project, which developed the first atomic bomb in nearby Los Alamos, originally used the Trujillo Plaza, at 109 East Palace, as a secret office in World War II.

Strolling along the river

Most great cities in the world were founded alongside great rivers or oceans. The Spanish forefathers placed Santa Fe on a river, but no one had illusions of grandeur about the little mountain creek. The Santa Fe River is as slow, irregular, and inexpedient as the town it crosses.

The creek was never a major factor in the development of the town, but it had a symbolic hold on the residents for many years. For one thing, it determined the pattern of the city's settlement. In the first two centuries new residents built streets and homes parallel to the course of the river, seldom more than a few blocks away from the water. In the early 19th century, when the Santa Fe Trail was opened, the city was described as "three streets wide and a mile long," following the path of the river.

The river also served in the first century of the city as the dividing line between social classes. The Spanish soldiers and priests lived north of the river, on the plaza side, and their Indian servants from Mexico lived on the south side. The Indians named their area *analco,* meaning the other side of the water.

The most important structure in the Barrio de Analco is the Chapel of San Miguel, built about 1610-1612 to serve as the mission church for the Indian servants. The Pueblos gutted the church and razed all of the homes in the Barrio during the 1680 Revolt. The residents who escaped the attack found safety in the Palace of the Governors and retreated to El Paso with the Spanish. Very few returned in the reconquest.

The Barrio was rebuilt in the early 18th century. It was no longer strictly a district for

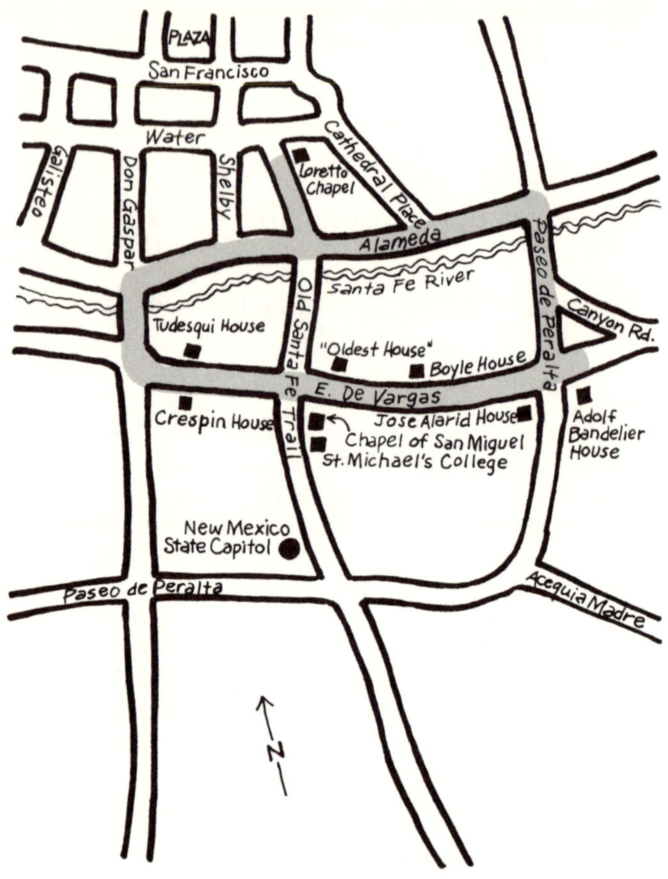

servants, but class associations lingered until the 19th century. Some of the lovely homes in the Barrio today were originally constructed for laborers and low-ranking soldiers.

The best place to enter the Barrio de Analco is the corner of Don Gaspar and East De Vargas, which can be reached by following the river west along Alameda Street from the bridge on Old Santa Fe Trail and going south on Don Gaspar a short block. East De Vargas was laid out in 1610 and still follows the same path as the original street.

Roque Tudesqui House (129-135 East De Vargas)

Roque Tudesqui was a successful trader in the early days of the Santa Fe Trail. He was Italian by birth, a rare nationality in Santa Fe at the time. He bought this house in 1841, when he was forty, shortly before his marriage to a local *senorita*.

There is no record of when the house was built, though there was a home on or near the site in the mid-18th century. The house is now divided into two private residences.

Gregorio Crespin House (132 East De Vargas)

General De Vargas granted this land to Juan de Leon Brito in the late 17th century, as a reward for service in the Spanish reconquest of Santa Fe. The house was built early in the following century, between 1720-1750 according to tree-ring specimens taken from the *vigas*. A deed from 1747 shows the property being sold by Gregorio Crespin for 50 *pesos*.

The house became larger over the years and certainly more valuable. In the mid-19th century it contained five rooms, all opening onto the portal by the garden. The territorial trim was added several decades later. The house remains a private residence today.

Chapel of San Miguel

The walls of the original Chapel, dating to the earliest years of the Spanish settlement, are still intact, but are not now visible. The Pueblos destroyed most of the church in the 1680 Revolt. When the Spanish rebuilt the Chapel in 1710, they altered the shape of the structure and put up new outer walls alongside the old ones.

The Spanish were more cautious about Indian raids in 1710 than they had been in 1610 and restored the Chapel as a fortress. In addition to the thick walls, they placed the windows high on the building and added adobe battlements to the roof. The roof line was altered again the next century with the addition of a triple-tiered tower, which was displaced by the current square tower in the 1870s.

Used originally as the mission church for the Mexican Indian servants in the Barrio de Analco, the rebuilt Chapel served the Spanish military in the 18th century. The Christian Brothers acquired the church in the mid-19th century for the adjacent school that they operated until recently. The Brothers still staff and maintain the Chapel.

The most prominent feature of the interior is the fine *reredo*, or altar screen. Made in 1798, it was designed to display the small gilded statue of St. Michael, the patron of the Chapel, and the six attached paintings. The statue, probably created in Mexico in the 17th century, was taken in procession throughout the frontier colony in 1709 to raise money, goods, and services for the restoration of the Chapel. Fundraising techniques were quite different in the days before grant applications.

Most of the paintings on the altar screen were done in Mexico in the 18th century. From left to right and top to bottom, the paintings depict St. Theresa of Avila, St. Michael, St. Gertrude, St. Francis of Assisi, Jesus, and St. Louis. The paintings hanging midway down the nave were done by early Franciscan missionaries to illustrate the Bible to the Indians. The one showing Christ on the cross is on buffalo hide and the other, of Christ the Good Shepherd, is on deer skin.

The old bell displayed in the gift shop, which once hung in the tower, was made in 1856. Defects in the sand-casting make the date appear to be 1356, but it is not medieval.

St. Michael's College

Just south of the Chapel on Old Santa Fe Trail is the building used by the Christian Brothers for many years as St. Michael's College. The Brothers sold the property in 1965 to the State of New Mexico, which has named it the Lamy Building and uses it for state offices.

At the time of construction, in 1878, it was the largest and highest adobe structure in Santa Fe. Originally there was a third story, destroyed by fire in the 1920s, which served as the college dormitory. The surviving stories of the building housed administration and classroom space.

The Christian Brothers founded the college in 1859, on instructions from Bishop Lamy, as a school for boys, providing formal secondary and college education for the first time in the area. In 1947 the Brothers separated the high school and college levels, establishing the College of Santa Fe and St. Michael's High School, both now located in other areas of town.

New Mexico State Capitol

Farther south on Old Santa Fe Trail is an unusual state capitol. The architects, shunning typical capitol facades, designed the building in the general shape of a Pueblo *kiva* and then tried to make it look official with territorial trim. The result is a little silly, but not for that reason inappropriate for the building's use.

The "Oldest House" (215 East De Vargas)

Pueblo Indians may have laid the original foundations for this building in the 13th century, though the *vigas* in the current ceiling, according to tree-ring specimens, go back only to about 1750. Whatever the original building date, and the accuracy of the claim to being "the oldest house in the United States," the western portion is a good example of old adobe construction. Most Santa Fe residents lived in similar rooms in the early centuries, part Indian and part Spanish in architecture, with low, log ceilings, dirt floors, thick adobe walls, and a corner fireplace for heating and cooking. The walls are made of poured mud instead of adobe bricks, a once-typical technique called "puddling."

The house is open to the public. The eastern portion is used as an Indian crafts shop.

Boyle House (327 East De Vargas)

The Boyle family acquired the house in the 1880s in two different purchases. For some years previous, ownership of the house had been divided between two families, separated by a central hallway. At various times before then, the house belonged to the Catholic Church, U.S. soldiers, and a family of prominent Spanish landowners.

The age of the building is unknown, but it is probably as old as most of the structure of the "oldest house." It existed for certain by the 1760s, and the four-foot-thick walls suggest the possibility of an earlier origin.

Jose Alarid House (338 East De Vargas)

Jose Alarid, a disabled veteran, built this house in the late years of Mexican rule in Santa Fe. He sold the property in 1854 and it changed hands a number of times after that. At one point Bishop Lamy owned the house for five years, though he probably never lived in it.

A later owner, Anita Chapman, was the first woman to serve as Territorial Librarian.

Her immediate successors in the office were also women, which caused a legal controversy in the early 20th century. The state Supreme Court was asked to decide whether a woman could serve in a public position in New Mexico. In a split decision, the Court ruled that the office of Librarian did not require "judgment in any respect" and so the duties "are not incompatible with the ability of a woman to perform."

The house is now occupied by the Mudd-Carr Gallery.

Adolph Bandelier House (352 East De Vargas)

Adolph Bandelier rented the house during his ten-year stay in Santa Fe in the 1880s. Bandelier, an internationally-known Swiss scholar, was the first outsider to understand the historical and anthropological significance of the Santa Fe area and to write about it for other outsiders. His research on the Pueblos, which involved living in Indian villages for weeks at a time and traveling thousands of miles on foot and horseback, resulted in a novel called *The Delight Makers*. He wrote scientific papers as well, but had the good sense to realize that his findings were only tentative and best expressed as fiction. The novel is ponderous, but definitely worth reading for imaginative insights about the early Pueblos.

Later owners of the house may be better known locally then Bandelier. Santa Fe merchant Henry Kaune, whose wife was Bandelier's niece, bought it in 1919. The Kaunes established a popular local grocery in Santa Fe, still thriving today.

Browsing along the way

The Mudd-Carr Gallery, in the Jose Alarid house, carries an excellent selection of Indian and Spanish crafts. Nambe Mills, a local manufacturer of distinctive metal cooking and serving ware, has a showroom on Paseo de Peralta, on the other side of Alameda Street. West along the river, back on Old Santa Fe Trail, is the Inn at Loretto, where the Golden Bough, The Santa Fe Store, and several other fine shops are located. Next to the Inn is the beautiful Loretto Chapel.

Loretto Chapel (219 Old Santa Fe Trail)

The Sisters of Loretto built the Chapel of Our Lady of Light in the 1870s to serve the girls school that they operated on the present site of the Inn at Loretto. When the boys of St. Michael's College, right down the street, were worshipping at the Chapel of San Miguel, the girls of Loretto Academy were here.

The small Gothic chapel, modeled on St. Chapelle in Paris, was designed by one of the French architects who was building St. Francis Cathedral at the same time. John Lamy, nephew of the bishop, shot and killed the architect, on suspicion of adultery with his wife, before the plans were completed. The construction crew could not figure out how the architect intended to build a stairway to the choir loft, since there did not seem to be room for it. They built a loft but finished the job without providing any means of reaching it. The Sisters were distressed, of course, and prayed for the help of St. Joseph, a carpenter by trade. Before long a carpenter appeared and constructed the circular "miraculous staircase" without using nails or any visible means of support. Local legend attributes the work to St. Joseph because the carpenter disappeared, without pay or even thanks, as soon as he completed his masterpiece.

Canyon Road

Canyon Road is one of the most romantic and picturesque streets in the United States, and certainly the oldest one still in use. The Pueblo Indians established it as a trail at least a century before any Europeans arrived to stay in the American hemisphere. The trail, which ran the same course as the current paved street, followed the Santa Fe river over the Sangre de Cristo Mountains to the Pecos Pueblo. The Spanish *Conquistadores* maintained it for the same purpose, calling it *el camino de Canon.*

By the early 18th century the Spanish were building homes and cultivating fields along Canyon Road. Sections of some of the current buildings date from that period, and the style of the street's architecture was established in a way that has not changed substantially since then. The old adobes that line the narrow, winding street are built almost flush with the pavement, giving the walker at some points the feeling of being channeled through an adobe tunnel. The plain-looking facades along the street present a deceptive impression about what is inside. The homes were built around a central patio, or *placita.* As families grew and children started their own families, new rooms and separate buildings were added around the *placita,* producing rambling structures and compounds which are only partially visible from the street. Since the patio was the center of family and social life, landscaping was reserved for that area and the finest architectural details face inwardly around it, blocked away from the dust and noise of the street by the front facade. Twentieth-century American settlers in Santa Fe, unable to give up front yards altogether, have modified the

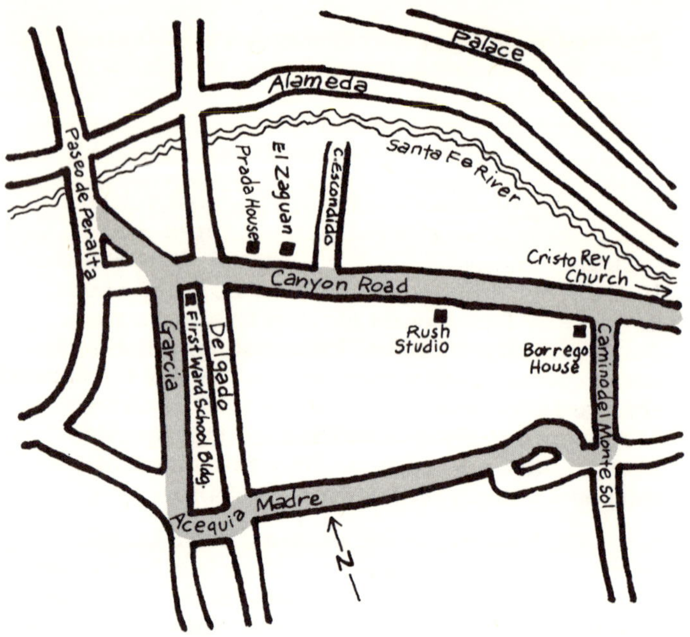

style on nearby streets by building adobe walls right up to the pavement, creating a similar sense of hidden charm.

Early this century Canyon Road became the center of the Santa Fe art colony. Not as many artists live and work there today as in the past — too expensive — but it has retained its artistic character. City zoning designates it as a "residential arts and crafts zone," limiting its use to residences, studios, art galleries, crafts shops, restaurants, and related neighborhood services. It's an ideal place for exploring both the residential character of the old city and the latest work of Southwestern artists.

First Ward School Building (400 Canyon Road)

The difficulty that modern ways have encountered in Santa Fe is aptly illustrated in this structure. When it was built in 1906, it was a symbol of progress in two important respects. It was, for one thing, constructed with kilned bricks rather than adobe blocks. The bricks were standardized and regular in form, unlike the adobes, and much easier to maintain, which seemed at the time to give them destiny's edge. Also, it was built as a public school, which the city leaders expected to rapidly displace the existing church schools established by Bishop Lamy. Neither expectation was fulfilled.

The Board of Education sold it in 1928. Since then it has been a movie theater for foreign films, a residence, an antique shop, and once even a zoo for indigenous birds and animals. Today it serves modernity again, more successfully, as the home of the Linda Durham Gallery.

Juan Jose Prada House (519 Canyon Road)

Early maps of Santa Fe indicate that this house existed before the Boston Tea Party, though written records go back only to the years right after the Civil War. In the 1860s, when it was the residence of Juan Jose Prada, it was divided into two sections, separated by a central corridor. Prada sold the west section in 1869 and his widow deeded the east section to her daughter and son-in-law in 1882. Both deeds stipulated that the front door of the corridor, facing the street, be left open for access to a dance hall in the rear of the house.

The dance hall was gone when Mrs. Charles Dietrich purchased the property about 50 years ago and joined the two sections. One of the pioneers of historic preservation in Santa Fe, Mrs. Dietrich lived in the house for many years and was instrumental in saving other old Canyon Road homes from destruction. The building is still a private residence.

Behind the house is one of the few surviving examples of the New Mexico equivalent of frontier log cabins. From the earliest Spanish days inhabitants used *jacal* construction for some purposes, particularly for outbuildings. The small barn on the Prada property is typical, with squared-off cedar logs set upright in the ground, the cracks filled with adobe. *Jacal* buildings could be as solid and well insulated as most log cabins, but they were seldom used as residences because of the superior protection provided by thick adobe walls.

El Zaguan (545 Canyon Road)

This rambling old *hacienda* is one of the architectural treasures of Santa Fe. When James Johnson bought it in 1849, it consisted of two or three rooms, built at an uncertain earlier date with four-foot-thick walls.

Johnson was a prominent merchant in the days of the Santa Fe Trail. He operated a general store on the northeast corner of the plaza, bringing in his merchandise by wagon train across the Trail from Missouri. Behind the house, in addition to an orchard and cornfield, he built large corrals for the oxen and horses used on the long trek.

Johnson enlarged the house considerably and converted it to territorial style, noticeable from the street by the brick coping on the roof. The new rooms, with walls only three feet thick, included a "chocolate room,"' where chocolate was ground and served each afternoon, a private chapel, and a library that contained the largest collection of books in New Mexico at the time. At one point there were 24 rooms, even with the servants quartered across the street. As the house grew, so did its *zaguan,* the covered passageway which runs its full length in the back and has given the house its name.

Adolph Bandelier, the pioneering anthropologist, designed the garden west of the house in the 1880s. The two chestnut trees, which have become city landmarks, were already there at the time, but Bandelier brought in the peony bushes from China that are still flourishing a hundred years later.

Among the buildings saved from destruction by Mrs. Charles Dietrich in the 1920s and 30s, the property is now owned by the Historic Santa Fe Foundation. Inside it has been converted into rental apartments of various sizes, but the exterior has been preserved.

Olive Rush Studio (630 Canyon Road)

Olive Rush was well known as an artist within the Society of Friends (the Quakers). She first visited Santa Fe in 1914 and moved to the town in 1920, the first woman to join the budding art colony.

Rush made her home and studio in this old adobe, which had been in the Sena and Rodriguez families for generations before. The house was probably built in the first half of the 19th century, judging by the thickness of the walls, the side portal, and the back garden. Records from those days are not very informative. There were no surveys and deeds were seldom filed. Families held the same property for generations and knew its boundaries by birthright. When they attempted to describe property on paper, the accounts were usually confusing and inaccurate, particularly along Canyon Road.

Rush preserved the house in its original state. The Society of Friends, who now use it as a meeting-house, has maintained it with the same degree of care.

Browsing along the way

The galleries and shops along Canyon Road are particularly strong in Spanish antiques and

20th century art. The Linda McAdoo Gallery, the Munson Gallery, and the Canyon Road Art Gallery carry a significant range of representational paintings. The Graphics House handles nice lithographs, and Running Ridge features fine crafts as well as prints. Linda Durham has the best selection of contemporary art on the street.

For Spanish colonial antiques, the choices include Jeffrey Adams Antiques, Robert Nichols', La Bodega, Claiborne Gallery, Architectural Antiques, and Southwest Spanish Craftsmen.

Borrego House (724 Canyon Road)

This is one of the few houses on Canyon Road which can be traced with Spanish deeds. A smaller version of the house existed in 1753, when it was sold as part of a farm. The farm, like others nearby, extended south from the street a few hundred yards to the *acequia madre*, the source of irrigation water.

The Borrego family owned the home for 75 years in the 19th century. They added the large front room, for political and social entertaining, and the territorial-style portal along the street. They also left posterity some incredible deed tangles. The original purchaser, Rafael Borrego, willed half of the property to his widow and half to his children. From then until 1939, various parts of the house were owned by different people, sometimes not of the same family. By the time that Raphael's widow died in 1872, the Borregos were deeding individual rooms, a fairly common practice in Santa Fe before the 20th century. There were even cases where parts of a room were bequeathed to heirs.

Mrs. Charles Dietrich purchased all of the rooms between 1928 and 1939, and restored the house carefully. The property has changed ownership several times since then, but has been used as a restaurant for many years now.

Camino del Monte Sol

The street just beyond the Borrego House, Camino del Monte Sol, is almost as famous for its artists as Canyon Road. *Los Cinco Pintores* (the five painters), along with several other painters and writers, built homes on the *camino* early this century. Before then the undeveloped street was called Telephone Road, but the artists found the designation offensive and renamed it after nearby Sun Mountain.

One block along Camino del Monte Sol is Acequia Madre, which is a pleasant street to follow back towards downtown. There is, however, another important sight a few blocks farther up Canyon Road.

Cristo Rey Church

The church houses the most famous piece of Spanish colonial art in New Mexico, an ornately-carved stone *reredo*, or altar screen, commissioned in 1760. Originally made for the military chapel, *La Castrense*, which once stood on the plaza, the *reredo* became a model for many later hand-hewn wooden altar screens in New Mexico. Depicted on the intricate baroque *reredo*, from top to bottom and left to right, are God, Our Lady of Valvanera, St. John Nepomuk, St. James the Apostle, St. Joseph, St. Ignatius Loyola, and St. Francis of Solano.

The church was built in 1940 to commemorate the 400th anniversary of Coronado's expedition into New Mexico. Architect John Gaw Meem designed it in classical Spanish mission style. Nearly 200,000 adobe bricks were used in the construction, all made from the soil on the site, which is the traditional practice. Parishioners contributed much of the labor, working under professional supervision.

Meem scaled the church, one of the largest

adobe structures in existence, to fit the great *reredo.* After *La Castrense* was demolished, Bishop Lamy concealed the altar screen behind a wall in the Cathedral. The French prelate disliked local religious art, particularly in his Romanesque church. Meem gave the work a much more proper home.

Acequia Madre

The only remaining *acequia,* or irrigation ditch, in Santa Fe is the *acequia madre* — mother ditch — which flows along the street that bears its name, and is still used to water gardens and trees near its path. Before Santa Fe knew the technology of deep wells and running water, the *acequias* were an essential part of the town's life. They carried melting snow from the mountains into the fields and orchards of the village during the growing season, when rainfall was undependable. Without the *acequias* the area would have been uninhabitable. They are still a cherished and practical part of life along Acequia Madre and north of Santa Fe in rural areas and small towns.

The Pueblos used ditch irrigation at least 1,000 years ago, but the Spanish knew it, too, before their arrival and had developed an elaborate system of irrigation law. The law provided rights of ownership to shares of water from the ditch. Larger fields got larger proportions of the water. Generally water rights were transferred along with land, but owners could lose their rights by not contributing adequately to the maintenance of the ditches. The annual cleaning of the ditches, supervised by the *mayordomo de la acequia,* was an important community activity. Everyone with water rights worked together to clear the ditch of winter debris from its source down to the last farm. On Acequia Madre, and all across the northern part of New Mexico, the system is still firmly in place today.

The street which runs along the mother ditch is one of the most pleasant in the city. The houses are not as historic as those on Canyon Road, but among the old trees and ample gardens, they gracefully reflect the historic character of the city.

Browsing along the way

Near the end of Acequia Madre are two art galleries which offer a wonderful contrast of styles. Both occupy superb exhibition spaces and feature excellent work, though their styles in each respect are very different. Heydt/Bair, on the corner of Garcia Street, represents contemporary artists in the area. The Fenn Gallery, on Pasco de Peralta, carries more traditional work, some from the Southwest and some from other places.

Garcia Street

The walk back to Canyon Road along Garcia Street passes through another attractive residential area. The homes on the tree-lined street are of a relatively recent vintage in Santa Fe terms, but they sit in their historic environment with as much harmony, comfort, and lack of pretense as the older homes nearby.

The high road to Taos

When the Spanish arrived in New Mexico to stay in the 17th century, some of the more independent and adventurous settlers pushed on beyond Santa Fe to the north. They established farms on both sides of the Rio Grande Valley, all along the 75-mile stretch between Santa Fe and the large Indian pueblo in Taos. Santa Fe was a small, isolated frontier village in this period, but compared to the northern settlements, it was a busy, cosmopolitan metropolis. A common punishment for crimes in Santa Fe in the early centuries was banishment to one or another of these remote villages, where life was invariably hard and lean.

Santa Fe courts no longer exile convicts to Chimayo or Las Trampas, but little else has changed substantially. If anything, survival may be tougher today in the northern villages than it was in the 17th and 18th centuries, and they have certainly lost ground to Santa Fe in contact with the outside world. Taos is, and always has been, a special case among the northern communities, but the others remain frontier outposts of the old world, rustic, pastoral, and still thoroughly Spanish.

Two recent books provide wonderful insights into their struggle against "progress." Robert Coles, in *The Old People of New Mexico*, describes the persistence of traditional values and mores in the villages. Taos writer John Nichols creates a fictional but authentic mountain community, populated with splendid characters, in *The Milagro Beanfield War*, one of the most delightful American novels of the 1970s.

The high road to Taos from Santa Fe passes

through several of the old world villages. The mountain scenery is spectacular, and Taos is a very nice destination, but the towns along the way are the unique part of the trip.

Chimayo

Chimayo is a major center of Spanish weaving in New Mexico. Families like the Ortegas and the Trujillos have been weaving in Chimayo for centuries. They developed a design pattern many years ago, named for the village, that is characterized by a background of one solid color, with stylized diamond figures in the center and stripes on the ends in different colors. The best place to see examples of the weaving today is at the Ortega family shop, where artisans work daily at their looms. The Ortegas stopped using home-spun yarn in the 1930s, and now employ some weavers from outside of the family, but the essence of their craft hasn't changed much since the 18th century.

The major attraction in Chimayo is the Santuario, a small chapel that is one of the most special places in the Southwest. The facade and the religious folk art inside are simple and unpolished, but intensely expressive, typical of Spanish frontier churches of the early 19th century.

The ground on which the chapel is built is reputed to have miraculous healing powers. Pilgrims visit Chimayo as they go to Lourdes in France, to cure their afflictions through faith. In a tiny back room, left of the altar, they crouch over a hole in the middle of the floor and take holy earth to apply to their bodies. In an adjoining room many of the cured have left their crutches, leg braces, and other testimonies of their faith.

Other kinds of pilgrims look for their succor at the Rancho de Chimayo, one of the best-known restaurants in New Mexico. Housed in a lovely adobe *hacienda*, not far from the Santuario, the Rancho serves some of the most authentic traditional cooking in the state.

Cordova

Cordova is a few miles east of Chimayo, just off the high road in a heavily-tilled valley. It is known primarily for its woodcarving, particularly a style of carefully incised, unpainted *santos* named for the village.

The founder of the modern carving tradition in Cordova was Jose Dolores Lopez, born in 1868. Like his father before him, Lopez was a carpenter and furniture-maker by trade who used his skills in his free time to help beautify the local church. During World War I, anxious about a son who had been drafted, Lopez began carving small wooden figures, mainly animals, for relaxation. Members of the Santa Fe art colony "discovered" his work shortly afterwards and convinced Lopez that he should begin making some carvings to sell, which must have been a startling idea in Cordova at the time. Lopez taught his techniques to his children, including the talented George Lopez, and they in turn have passed them on to grandchildren like Gloria Lopez Cordova and Eluid L. Martinez.

Truchas, Las Trampas, and Penasco

Truchas, the next community along the high road, has magnificent views across hundreds of miles of mountain and desert. A weaving center, like Chimayo, the design patterns of Truchas vary a little from the Chimayo style. Local weavers, such as the Cordova family, generally use a design scheme called Vallero, developed about a century ago by the Montoya sisters in the nearby town of El Valle.

Las Trampas is the site of a beautiful Spanish colonial chapel, San Jose de Gracias, built in the mid-18th century. The chapel is usually locked, but local residents can find the key. The religious folk art of the interior is superb.

At Penasco the high road goes east several miles along a fertile valley and then turns north for Taos on Route 3. Close to Penasco is Picuris Pueblo, founded in the late 13th century. One of the more pleasant pueblos to visit, Picuris has a small museum, ancient ruins, and even camping facilities.

Taos

The high road connects with Highway 68, the main route between Santa Fe and Taos, in the town of Ranchos de Taos, home of one of the most photographed churches in the United States. Though the St. Francis of Assisi Mission is a small chapel, it has massive adobe walls and buttresses which cast grand shadows in the New Mexico sun.

Just north on 68 is the downtown plaza of Taos. The Spanish founded the town around the plaza in 1617, less than a decade after the establishment of Santa Fe. The plaza has been the center of community life since, but its historic character has been obscured in recent years. In one of the country's most unfortunate tributes to the Bicentennial, Taos terraced its plaza with brick.

Near the plaza are several museums and historic homes. East one block is the home of Taos' best-known resident, Kit Carson. The famous scout, whose life was romanticized in the dime novels of the 19th century, lived here for 24 years. His home is now open as a museum.

North of the plaza one block is the home of Charles Bent, the first U.S. Territorial Governor of New Mexico. Shortly after his appointment, Bent was killed at home in a local uprising against American rule. Artifacts of the early

Southwest are displayed in the house today.

The Harwood Foundation Museum and Library is south of the plaza on Le Doux Street. The Museum has an extensive collection of paintings by founders of the Taos art colony as well as old Spanish furniture and crafts from the area. Next door is the home of Ernest Blumenschein, one of the best-known painters represented in the Harwood collection.

Paintings of a different sort, done by D.H. Lawrence, are exhibited in the manager's office of La Fonda Hotel, directly on the plaza. The Stables Gallery, one block north, shows work of members of the Taos Art Association. Behind it is the Clay and Fiber Gallery, which carries fine crafts. Other major downtown galleries include the Tally Richards Gallery of Contemporary Art at Placitas and Le Doux, the Magic Mountain Gallery and Galeria Nativa on the plaza, and DEL Galleries, Julia Black Gallery, and Mission Gallery on Kit Carson Road.

The other major attractions of Taos are away from the plaza, north of town. In addition to the pueblo, there is the ski basin, the Millicent Rogers Museum, and the D.H. Lawrence Ranch and Shrine. The Museum, located about one-half mile off of Route 3, near the intersection with the road to the ski basin, has an outstanding collection of Southwestern Indian and Spanish art. Lawrence's Ranch is about 15 miles farther, at the end of a scenic but rough mountain road that connects to Route 3. The Shrine, where Lawrence's ashes are interred, is open to visitors.

Taos Pueblo

The most impressive place in Taos is the pueblo. Virtually unchanged in appearance since the Spanish first saw it, it is the best preserved and most striking of all of the Indian pueblos in New Mexico.

Most of the residents continue to live in one of the two enormous adobe communal buildings, divided into many separate living spaces, which reach five stories into the sky. The mountain creek that runs between the two apartment compounds flows from sacred Blue Lake, high in the surrounding mountains. The river provides water for the community, which has spurned the installation of either water pipes or electricity.

Mountain trails

The mountain scenery around Santa Fe is some of the grandest in the Rockies. The peaks are higher in Colorado, the canyons are more colorful in Arizona, the wilderness area is larger in Idaho, the hot springs are more torrid in Wyoming, and the sky is bigger in Montana, but northern New Mexico is one of the few places in the Rocky Mountains where all of these natural features exist together. The total effect is spectacular, for hiking, skiing, camping, trail riding, fishing, or just taking a short drive from Santa Fe.

The best of the mountain scenery requires some exertion and preparation. Parts of the areas described below can be seen from a car, as in the case of the high road to Taos, but much more can be experienced on foot, hiking or skiing.

Hiking can be enjoyed most of the year, except after heavy snows. In any season hikers have to be prepared for extreme fluctuations in weather and temperature. Storms can move in very quickly, especially on summer afternoons. Hiking boots, water, and topographical maps are useful even for short walks and are necessary for longer ones. The local chapter of the Sierra Club has published a helpful guide for serious enthusiasts, *Day Hikes in the Santa Fe Area*, available in local book stores.

Northern New Mexico is popular for both downhill and cross-country skiing in the winter. The snow is usually deep and often powdery from December until Easter and the sun is more intense than anywhere else in the Rockies. The Santa Fe Ski Basin is the closest downhill area, less than an hour up a good road from the city. The Taos Ski Valley, about two hours away, is larger and has more exciting runs for advanced skiers. Both of these areas, and several others nearby, provide high altitude skiing, starting around 12,000 feet, with panoramic views of the mountains.

Opportunities for cross-country skiing are abundant. Some cross-country trails are mentioned below, but many more are described in Sam Beard's *Ski Touring in Northern New Mexico.* There are several places to rent equipment in both Santa Fe and Taos.

Horseback riding is a less strenuous means of mountain sightseeing. Both of the Tesuque resorts, Rancho Encantado and The Bishop's Lodge, allow non-guests on trail rides when there are extra horses available, though the chances of getting a mount are better at Double Arrow Stables on Old Santa Fe Trail. The trail rides stay at fairly low altitudes and don't allow much independent exploration, but the physical burden is shifted upward from the feet to more padded parts of the body.

Camping and fishing sites are scattered throughout the Santa Fe National Forest, which surrounds the city on three sides with a million and a half acres of mountain streams and lakes, backpacking opportunities, and campgrounds. The Forest Service sells an inexpensive map which indicates all of the possibilities and can provide current information at (505) 988-6643.

Hyde Memorial Park and the Santa Fe Ski Basin

The mountain access closest to Santa Fe is along the 17-mile road to the Santa Fe Ski Basin. The road climbs from 7,000 feet in town to 10,260 feet at the top, passing through a national forest and a state park. The views are wonderful from the road, particularly when the aspen are turning in the fall, but they only hint at what can be seen on the many foot trails nearby.

Several of the trails are relatively easy, short, and well marked. The Chamisa Trail starts five and a half miles from the beginning of the road, at the Forest Service sign indicating Trail #183. It climbs 700 feet through juniper, pine, and fir forests to a crest one and a quarter miles from the trailhead — a good spot for a picnic. Hikers can stop at the crest and return from there to the car, or can continue on the path downhill for another mile to a grassy meadow and the Big Tesuque Creek.

The Hyde Park Circle is a longer walk, about five miles, but no more strenuous. It begins at Hyde Park headquarters, directly across the road from the small general store. The trail, marked by three blazes (notches cut on trees), climbs steeply at first and then levels off gradually along a ridge. At the top are two picnic tables and a magnificent 360-degree view. Two paths lead back to the main road down the other side of the ridge. Just beyond the picnic tables is a branch of the trail jutting off to the right, a shorter but less scenic way down. The main trail goes straight at the junction. Both paths end at the Ski Basin road about one mile north of the park store.

Farther up the road are a number of longer and more difficult trails, two of which are excellent for cross-country skiing in the winter. One of the most beautiful at any time of the year follows the Aspen Vista Road to Tesuque Peak. The path starts at the Aspen Vista Picnic Area, a few miles below the Ski Basin. The sign saying "not for public use" applies only to vehicles. The first two and a half miles are through an aspen forest, gorgeous in the fall and wonderful for skiing in the winter. After crossing four forks of the Tesuque Creek, the trail heads up Tesuque Peak for three and a half miles through fir and spruce, affording fine views along the way of the Rio Grande Valley and Santa Fe. Even in mid-summer there is likely to be snow on the upper part of the trail before reaching the 12,040-foot summit.

The Winsor Trail is also good for both hiking and cross-country skiing. The trailhead is on the north side of the lower parking lot of the Ski Basin. It climbs abruptly at first through aspen and spruce for about half a mile. At the top is a meadow and a boundary fence for the Pecos Wilderness. From there the trail slopes gently downhill for about one and a half miles to the Rio Nambe. One route from this point is to follow the creek to the right about a mile and a half to Nambe Lake, though there is not a maintained trail in this direction. Most hikers stay on Winsor Trail to Puerto Nambe, another mile uphill. The ascent is steep, but offers grand views of Santa Fe Baldy, Lake Peak, and Penitente Peak. From the meadow at Puerto Nambe the Winsor Trail goes on to Spirit Lake, another two miles, and ultimately ends up near Cowles, on the other side of the range. Sky Line Trail goes off from Puerto Nambe to Lake Katherine and the summit of Santa Fe Baldy, three miles away.

Pecos Wilderness

The Pecos Wilderness can be entered by the Winsor Trail from the Ski Basin, but the most common approach is from N.M. 63. The highway starts about 20 miles east of Santa Fe, near the Pecos National Monument, a pueblo abandoned in the 1830s. A paved road follows the Pecos River north for 13 miles to the village of Tererro. Six miles farther on graded dirt is a junction where the town of Cowles used to be. Nearby are several national forest campgrounds which provide access to the wilderness.

Most of the marked trails in the area are strenuous and require a long day to enjoy fully. It's best to camp overnight or start very early in the morning from Santa Fe.

One of the most scenic trails goes to Pecos Baldy Lake and Peak. It starts at Jack's Creek Campground, three miles north of Cowles. It climbs steadily at first for 1,000 feet over two and a half miles. In a grassy meadow at that point, with beautiful distant views, the trail forks left. Over the next two miles the trail, marked occasionally by posts, goes through an aspen grove, another meadow, a pine forest, and then drops down to Jack's Creek. From the creek there is a steep two mile ascent through pines to the timber line and Pecos Baldy Lake. The summit of Pecos Baldy is 1,100 feet directly above the lake, another mile of hiking along the path through Horsethief Meadow.

Bandelier National Monument

Bandelier is one of the most special places in the Santa Fe area. The site of ancient Pueblo settlements, abandoned before the founding of Santa Fe, the park contains cliff dwellings, excavated and unexcavated ruins, sacred places, waterfalls, a small museum, complete camping facilities, a wilderness area for backpacking, and superb hiking trails. The areas most developed for sightseeing can be enjoyed on a half-day trip from Santa Fe, but there is enough of interest in the Monument to fill a week.

The 40-mile drive from Santa Fe is beautiful, particularly after leaving U.S. 84-285 and going west toward the Jemez Mountains on Route 4. Near the Rio Grande the road passes less than a mile from San Ildefonso Pueblo, always worth a detour, and then climbs the Pajarito Plateau. From the high spots on the plateau there are grand views eastward to the Sangre de Cristo Mountains, before the road descends into Frijoles Canyon and the park headquarters.

The primary ruins and cliff dwellings can be

seen on a short walk from the visitors' center, though serious hikers have lots of other options. A back country trail map is available at the visitors' center as well as a guide book about the trails. One of the best day hikes, covering 13 miles, goes to the Stone Lions Shrine, an ancient ceremonial carving which is still sacred to the Pueblos and is likely to be ringed with deer antler offerings. The hike is difficult at one point, but includes fine views of Frijoles Canyon from above, a range of vegetation, an unexcavated ruin, and 360-degree mountain panoramas.

Bandelier is open year-round, but fluctuations in the federal budget can affect some services. For current information on hours and facilities, call (505) 672-3861.

Other areas

There are numerous other exciting spots farther from Santa Fe in the mountains of northern New Mexico. North of the city on U.S. 84 is Ghost Ranch and the fabulous vistas painted there by Georgia O'Keeffe. Farther along the same highway are the towns of Tierra Amarilla, close to two recreational lakes, and Chama, originating point for narrow gauge rail trips on the Cumbres and Toltec Scenic Railroad.

Near Taos is the Rio Grande Gorge, a deep canyon that illustrates how mighty the river once was. The Rio Grande State Park is a good place to explore the canyon or fish the river, though the views are more dramatic from the bridge on U.S. 64. The beautiful drive to the Taos Ski Valley is north of the town, as is Wheeler Peak, the highest point in the state at 13,161 feet.

The area around Mora is fascinating, but not known well even in New Mexico. Settled by French trappers in the early 19th century, the tiny villages nearby, especially on Route 94, have not changed much since then. There is a splendid mountain drive from Mora through Guadalupita to Black Lake and the Angel Fire Ski Basin, unpaved for many miles and not shown on most maps.

West of Santa Fe, Route 4 passes through scenic sections of the Jemez Mountains. There is not much to see in Los Alamos, where the atomic bomb was developed, but farther along the road is the Valle Grande, an enormous caldera, or collapsed volcano. This is an excellent area for cross-country skiing or hiking in search of natural hot springs. An unpaved intersecting road, Route 126, crosses high country to Cuba, near the southern boundary of the Jicarilla Apache Reservation. Route 4 continues through Jemez Springs, with its roadside hot springs, and connects with Route 44, passing close to the Jemez, Zia, and Santa Ana Pueblos. Since Route 44 leads to Bernalillo, just north of Albuquerque, this can be a long but interesting way to reach Albuquerque from Santa Fe.

A shorter scenic route between the two cities is along the Turquoise Trail, which follows Route 14. The road passes by the old mining towns of Cerrillos, Madrid, and Golden, where the Pueblos mined turquoise in prehistoric times and where coal and gold have been sought in more recent centuries.

Festivals, fairs, and exhibits

During the summer Santa Fe becomes the arts capital of the United States. The abundance and excellence of performing arts events, combined with the plethora of visual arts shows, almost overwhelm the city of 50,000. Residents spend the rest of the year catching up from the extraordinary level of activity and the equally phenomenal influx of visitors who are attracted by it.

The Santa Fe Opera, performing one of the few summer seasons in the country, has earned critical acclaim around the world. The Museum of International Folk Art has achieved a similar status in its field, particularly with the recent acquisition of the Girard collection. The Santa Fe Chamber Music Festival, founded in 1973, is rapidly approaching the same recognition. The new Santa Fe Festival Theatre received more national attention in its first season, 1981, than many established theaters get in a decade.

The Santa Fe Film Festival opens the season in late April with a week of cinema. Artists from the National Theatre of Britain and the Dallas Ballet arrive a couple of months later to do training workshops and performances. Spanish Market and Indian Market, held on the plaza in July and August respectively, are major juried crafts fairs. Dozens of gallery openings sprinkle the season, which finally concludes in October with a visual arts celebration, the Santa Fe Festival of the Arts. The Museum of Fine Arts and the Armory for the Arts, which have exhibitions year-round, usually schedule one of their most significant shows for the October Festival.

Some Santa Fe residents dread the approach

of the summer season and its two million or so visitors, drawn in large part by the arts events. During the rest of the year Santa Fe is much more relaxed and secluded, closer to its historical character. But the excellence and cultural richness of the summer season cannot be denied. The city may become a little bloated with both genuine and phony sophistication, but Santa Fe also reaches a peak of artistry each summer that is a natural culmination of its remarkable cultural heritage.

The Santa Fe Opera

When John Crosby founded the Santa Fe Opera in 1957, opera in the United States was dominated by European talent and repetitive stagings of standard repertory. Crosby was convinced that opera could be more exciting, innovative, and American. He planned carefully for several years to create an outdoor summer festival which would feature and cultivate American musical talent. He chose Santa Fe for a location because most larger cities "have a great deal of rain, lots of mosquitos, and lots of airplanes overhead."

The original opera house was acoustically sound but not very grand, built at a cost of $115,000 to provide seating, on wooden benches, for 480 patrons. It burned during the eleventh season and was replaced by opening night of the next year, after a Gargantuan effort, with a magnificent new theater that can hold almost 1400 people comfortably. Placed in a large natural bowl in the Tesuque hills, just north of Santa Fe, the theater is open on the sides, and partially open on the top, to the resplendent evening skies. Even people who prefer different kinds of music attend the opera for its setting.

The productions are lavish and adventuresome. Most involve well over a hundred performers in the orchestra and chorus and are staged with imaginative flair in set and costume design. The emphasis is on new and neglected works. The annual season customarily includes some standard repertory, but the old warhorses are usually less exciting for the performers and the audience than the seldom-seen works. The Santa Fe Opera, despite its relative youth among major American companies, holds the national record for premieres, averaging one a summer.

The season opens in early July and runs until the end of August. In July performances are on Wednesdays, Fridays, and Saturdays; in August, Tuesday-Saturday. Admission is a bargain compared to opera prices in most cities, but is not cheap. For people on a tight budget, standing room is an incredible value, costing less than most movies.

Santa Fe Chamber Music Festival

Artistic Director Alicia Schachter, through her superb choice of musicians, and Festival Director Sheldon Rich, through aggressive determination, brought the Chamber Music Festival to national prominence very quickly. By the end of the Festival's first decade in 1982, it was being broadcast over National Public Radio, honored annually by Georgia O'Keeffe with stunning posters, and performing in post-season residencies each year in Seattle and New York City. Some critics feel that the Festival has begun to challenge the Opera for musical supremacy in the city.

As in the case of the Opera, the setting for performances is delightful. The Festival uses St. Francis Auditorium, in the Museum of Fine Arts, an intimate hall modeled on a Spanish mission chapel. The primary attraction, though, is the musical talent. Such eminent artists as violist Walter Trampler and pianist Andre-Michel Schub have participated several years each. Invariably, all of the artists have significant international credits and handle the diverse and difficult programming with mastery.

The five-week season runs from the middle of July to the middle of August. There are concerts on Sunday and Monday evenings and recitals on Thursdays. Additional events, including discussion rehearsals and special performances, are scheduled on most other days.

Bach Festival

Almost all of the musicians performing at the Opera and Chamber Music Festival come from outside of New Mexico. Professional local musicians don't get the festival stage until winter, when the Orchestra of Santa Fe produces its annual Bach Festival. Under the direction of William Kirschke the Orchestra has improved steadily for years and has become one of the best in its class in the country. In the weekend Festival, the Orchestra and the University of New Mexico Concert Choir perform work by all of the Bach family composers. After a day of skiing in February, the Festival provides the perfect transition back down from the summits.

The Santa Fe Festival Theatre

Three young theater professionals startled Santa Fe in 1981. Tom Gardner, Christopher Beach, and Robert Wojewodski first managed to get the state legislature to appropriate funds for the renovation of a theater—comparable to getting orange juice from a turnip—and then demonstrated abundant talent in their primary craft by producing three splendid plays in repertory. One of the productions, *Terra Nova*, a recent play by Ted Tally, was as finely honed as a surgeon's blade and as incisive. The first season was a convincing start, demonstrating that the

Festival Theatre was destined to become a major arts presence in Santa Fe.

Like the Opera and Chamber Music Festival, the Theatre employs talented artists from around the country who are attracted by the opportunity of spending the summer in Santa Fe. Sometimes they are well-known performers, such as Michael York, who came to play the lead in *Cyrano de Bergerac.* Most of the artists are less established in popular reputation, but all are experienced professionals, carefully selected for the repertory, who do not disappoint an audience.

Performances are held in the Armory for the Arts on most days in July and August.

British American Theatre Institute

The National Theatre of Britain, the prestigious London institution directed originally by Sir Lawrence Olivier, established the Institute in 1982 to provide professional training in the United States. Some of the leading artists in the National Theatre offer master classes for students selected by audition from throughout the country. The British artists also direct and perform in small-scale productions for the public, mounted without full sets or costumes. The performances are more than readings but less than completely-staged plays.

Performances are held at the Greer Garson Theatre on the campus of the College of Santa Fe in July and early August.

Dallas Ballet

The Dallas Ballet is planning to make Santa Fe its summer home. The Ballet began the move in 1981 by offering training workshops during July at the College of Santa Fe. By 1982 the company was also performing for one week, to live orchestra accompaniment, with the intention of expanding the season to the full month of July by 1986.

The Ballet is a young company, but has experienced leadership and has grown dynamically in the last few years. Flemming Flindt, formerly with the Royal Danish Ballet, is the artistic director.

Santa Fe Film Festival

Bill and Stella Pence, founders of the Telluride Film Festival, started a second, separate festival in Santa Fe in 1980. It differs from other cinema marathons in focusing each year on special themes, which have included such subjects as "New Directors/New Films," "The Western Film," and "Music and the Movies." In choosing films to document a theme, the Festival determines that a notable figure associated with each selected movie is able to attend.

The films are screened at the Lensic Theatre and the Armory for the Arts for a week in late April. The Festival has ambitious plans for a few years hence to take over all of the theaters in town for the week.

Spanish Market

The Spanish Colonial Arts Society sponsors an annual fair to recognize artistic achievement in traditional Spanish colonial crafts. Juries of experts give financial awards in the areas of woodcarving, weaving, *colcha* stitchery, jewelry, furniture, iron work, and straw inlay. The Market, held in the plaza on the last full weekend of July, is the best place in Santa Fe to see and buy a range of traditional Spanish crafts.

Indian Market

The Southwestern Association on Indian Affairs was formed in 1922 to defeat the Bursum

Bill, legislation that would have taken land and water rights from the Pueblos. The primary purpose of the Association today is the preservation and encouragement of Southwestern Indian arts, a goal addressed through Indian Market and other activities.

The Market is nationally recognized as a showplace for Indian art, contemporary as well as traditional. The Association's cash awards, given in a variety of fields, and the screening of work by the Standards Committee, maintain a high level of quality. There are over 300 exhibitors each year, mainly from Southwestern tribes.

The Market is held in the plaza on the third weekend of August.

Santa Fe Festival of the Arts

The Festival of the Arts is the only one of Santa Fe's festivals that was not begun by professionals in an arts field. Despite its origins in a Chamber of Commerce effort to promote tourism during October, it has grown considerably since 1977 in artistic integrity. During a ten-day period in October, the Festival sponsors a series of curated and juried exhibitions organized around different themes. Each show features some New Mexico artists and most of the shows come exclusively from within the state. The exhibitions are mounted at the Sweeney Convention Center, a converted high school gymnasium that is not ideal for much of anything, but is the largest possible space in town and is used well by the Festival.

Museum of International Folk Art

The Museum has the finest collection of international folk crafts in the world, and is one of the most delightful places to spend time in Santa Fe. The collection is particularly strong in regional Spanish folk art, but is very broad in scope, and deep in many other areas, too.

Florence Dibell Bartlett established the Museum, which opened in 1953, to house her collection. The recent acquisition of the Girard collection—more than 100,000 pieces of folk art gathered around the world by Alexander and Susan Girard—firmly solidifies the Museum's international standing.

The Museum is located on Camino Lejo, just off Old Santa Fe Trail, about two miles south of the plaza. It is open Tuesday-Saturday, 9:00 a.m.-4:45 p.m. It is a branch of the Museum of New Mexico, along with the Museum of Fine Arts and the Palace of the Governors, both described earlier as sights near the plaza.

Wheelwright Museum of the American Indian

Mary Cabot Wheelwright founded the Museum in 1937 to help preserve disappearing aspects of Navajo religion and ceremony. When the Navajos took up their own preservation efforts, much of the original collection was returned to them and the scope of the Museum was broadened. Exhibits today feature American Indian arts and artifacts from any period or place. The Museum shop downstairs, designed to resemble an old Navajo trading post, is almost as large and interesting as the exhibition area.

The Wheelwright is located on Camino Lejo, behind the Museum of International Folk Art, about two miles south of the plaza. It is open Monday-Saturday, 11:00 a.m.-5:00 p.m., and Sunday, 1:00-5:00 p.m.

Laboratory of Anthropology

The primary purpose of the Laboratory is to protect and preserve the Indian heritage in New Mexico. Before land can be developed in the state, the Laboratory has to certify through archaeological research that the site does not have historical significance. The Laboratory is also entrusted with the care of Indian art and artifacts belonging to the State. The exhibition of the collection is a secondary function at the Laboratory, but the exhibits, featuring Pueblo and Navajo work, are certainly worth seeing.

The Laboratory is located on Camino Lejo, next to the Museum of International Folk Art, about two miles south of the plaza. It is open Monday-Friday, 9:00 a.m.-4:45 p.m.

El Rancho de las Golondrinas

The Ranch of the Swallows is a large, well-restored Spanish colonial estate on the outskirts of Santa Fe. It is maintained by a private foundation as a living museum of the Spanish colonial heritage.

The ranch includes homes built in the 17th and 18th centuries, agricultural buildings, several water mills, blacksmithing and wheelwrighting facilities, and a winery. Also on the grounds are interesting re-creations of an old Spanish mountain village, typical of rural life north of Santa Fe in earlier years, and a *morada,* a special kind of chapel used by Penitentes in flagellation rites.

The ranch is open for self-guided tours on the first Sunday of June, July, August, and September from 10:00 a.m.-4:00 p.m. There are guided tours on Wednesdays and Saturdays in June, July, and August at 10:00 a.m., and groups can arrange special tours at other times between April 1 and October 31 by calling 471-2261 well in advance.

The best times to visit are during the spring and fall festivals, usually held on the first weekends of May and October. On these occasions local Spanish artists demonstrate colonial crafts and perform traditional folk music and dances. On festival weekends there is not a more fascinating place in the area.

El Rancho is located in La Cienega, which can be reached by an exit on Interstate 25, a few miles south of the Santa Fe city limits.

Armory for the Arts

Artists developed this old national guard armory into an arts center during the 1970s. The place was a mess when they started and the transformation was gradual, but the result is impressive. During the summer it serves as the home of the Santa Fe Festival Theatre. In other seasons local performing artists and producers rent the theater for a variety of events. The lobby is a functional and spacious exhibition area, usually showing the work of local artists who are not yet well known.

The Armory is located at 1050 Old Pecos Trail, about one and a half miles from the plaza. The gallery is open Monday-Friday, 9:00 a.m.-5:00 p.m., except during lunch. Call 988-1886 for information on current shows.

School of American Research

Open to visitors only by appointment, the School has an outstanding collection of Southwestern Indian art and crafts, particularly modern work. Call 982-3584 for appointments, Monday-Friday.

The School has been an important force in Santa Fe life most of the 20th century. The Archaeological Institute of America established it as a research center in 1907 to further the study of American prehistory. Anthropologists working at the School stirred up considerable local and national interest in the Southwestern heritage, encouraging preservation efforts in Santa Fe and the growth of tourism.

The School was instrumental in the development of the Museum of New Mexico and was housed for many years in the Palace of the Governors. In 1972 the School moved to its present headquarters in a lovely residential compound at 660 East Garcia Street.

San Ildefonso Pueblo Museum

San Ildefonso, home of famous potter Maria Martinez, is the only pueblo near Santa Fe with its own museum. The Museum and its collection are both small, but impressive for the size of the community.

Indian work can also be seen in two shops in the village, the Popovi Da Studio of Indian Arts and the Aguilar Shop. The Popovi Da Studio was founded by Maria Martinez's son and daughter-in-law and contains, in addition to the shop, a small gallery of Maria's work that is open to Indian visitors.

Fiestas

Most of the Spanish and Pueblo towns of New Mexico have an annual fiesta to celebrate their existence as communities. The fiestas are similar in some respects to annual festivities of other towns in the country—county fairs, founder's day events, Oktoberfests, and the plethora of other occasions used by communities to reaffirm a local heritage.

The most traditional of the New Mexico fiestas are a special category of these events. Scheduled to commemorate the patron saint of the town or an important historical event, fiestas involve moments of solemnity as well as play. The activities always include ceremonial pageants of some kind, usually ancient in origin. Most fiestas involve lots of food, and are even called Feast Days in the pueblos. When some sort of trading or commercial exchange goes on, it is a secondary function to the rest of the activities. Fiestas are staged for residents, almost all of whom participate in some way, and not for visitors, though they are frequently the most interesting time of the year to visit New Mexico towns.

In addition to the Feast Days, the pueblos of the area have a variety of other ceremonial community events, some scheduled annually and some not scheduled on any regular basis. Almost weekly there is something happening in one or more of the pueblos, whether planned in advance or not. Visitors are allowed to attend many of the ceremonies, though not all, as long as they maintain respect for religious rites and strictly observe local laws. The laws prohibit drinking or approaching a *kiva* and generally preclude photography or sketching.

The following calendar provides dates and brief descriptions of traditional fiestas and other community celebrations. To learn about Pueblo activities planned for dates not listed, call the Eight Northern Indian Pueblos Council (505-852-4265) and the Six Sandoval Indian Pueblos, Inc. (505-465-2255), or the governor's office of a particular pueblo. Most ceremonial days begin about mid-morning and continue until sunset, with the exceptions noted.

January

6	Celebration of King's Day, involving the installation of the pueblo governor and council members. Eagle, Elk, Buffalo, and Deer dances are common. Observed by most of the pueblos.
23	San Ildefonso Feast Day. Begins with vespers on the evening before, followed by a procession around the plaza and dances by the Game Priest, Buffalo Woman, Buffalo, and Deer. On Feast Day morning these dancers appear again at dawn, coming out of the hills east of the village. After more dancing there is mass, another procession, and then dancing again.

February

2	Celebration of Candelaria Day at Picuris, Santo Domingo, and San Felipe with Buffalo and other dances.
A weekend	Hopi Bean dance. The date varies for this ancient tribute to the bean.

March

19	St. Joseph's Feast Day at Laguna. Harvest dance.

April

Easter	Various dances at many of the pueblos.

May

1	San Felipe Feast Day in honor of the local patron saint. Mass is early in the morning, followed by a procession which carries an image of St. Phillip from the church to a shrine in the plaza. Ritual clowns circle the pueblo, chanting and shaking rattles, and then lead the Corn dance. Afterwards, there is more dancing in front of the plaza shrine, a mid-afternoon feast, and a final procession to return the image of the saint to the church.
3	Celebration of Santa Cruz Day at Taos and Cochiti. Corn dances and other activities.

June

13	Sandia Feast Day in honor of St. Anthony, the community's patron saint. Features the Corn dance. San Ildefonso, San Juan, Santa Clara, and Taos also celebrate St. Anthony's Day with the Corn dance.
24	San Juan Feast Day in honor of the local patron saint, St. John the Baptist. Begins with vespers and a Buffalo dance on the evening of the 23rd. The major ceremony on Feast Day is the Comanche dance, about noon. Taos and Cochiti also celebrate St. John's Day, with the Corn dance at Taos and Grab Day at Cochiti.
29	Celebration of San Pedro's Day at San Felipe, Santa Ana, and Santo Domingo. Corn dances.

July

2nd week-end	Espanola Fiesta. Features parades, historical pageantry, food booths, and entertainment on the plaza.
14	Cochiti Feast Day in honor of St. Bonaventure. An early mass precedes a procession carrying an image of the saint from the church to a shrine in the plaza. Ritual clowns move around the village, chanting and shaking rattles, and lead the Corn dance. After more dancing and feasting the day ends with a final procession about 6:00 p.m.
3rd week-end	Chimayo's Fiesta de Santiago. Mass, food, and entertainment at Holy Family Church.
25	Celebration of St. James' Day. Grab Day at San Felipe, Acoma, Cochiti, Laguna, and Santo Domingo. People with the same name as the saint throw food from the top of houses.
26	Santa Ana Feast Day in honor of St. Anne, the community's patron saint. Mass, processions, the Corn dance, and Horse dancers.
Last week-end	Santa Clara's Puye Cliffs Ceremonial. Dances by Santa Clara, Nambe, and San Ildefonso Pueblos at ancestral ruins. The Puye Cliffs are a grand spot for the Ceremonial.

August

2	Old Pecos Bull Dance at Jemez, in celebration of Our Lady of the Angels, patron of the extinct Pecos Pueblo, whose survivors now live at Jemez. The Pecos Bull appears in the late afternoon of August 1, in the form of a man

wearing a wooden frame covered with black cloth and a roll of sheepskin for a head. The bull charges around the village, pursued by boys in blackface. Ritual clowns appear later and chant their way around the village. The next morning, after mass, the bull leads a procession to the plaza and engages in more play with the blackface boys. The Corn dance follows in the afternoon.

4 Santo Domingo Feast Day in honor of patron St. Dominic. After early mass a procession carries an image of the saint to a shrine in the plaza. Ritual clowns, decorated with body paint and corn husks in their hair, move around the village. The Corn dance is the largest in any of the pueblos, involving some 500 dancers. The day concludes close to sunset with a procession back to the church, returning the image of St. Dominic. This is one of the best-known and well-attended pueblo fiestas.

10 Picuris Feast Day in honor of patron San Lorenzo. Begins with a Sunset dance on the evening of the 9th. Feast Day opens with mass and a procession, which is followed by a ceremonial relay race, with racers wearing breechcloths and body paint. There is dancing in mid-afternoon and then a pole climb, when participants scale a 40-foot-high pole to retrieve a sheep carcass on top. The Picuris clowns are dressed colorfully in skull caps with corn-husks and necklaces of plastic fruit or glazed doughnuts. In nearby Penasco there is a carnival on the same day. Acoma honors St. Lawrence with the Corn dance and Laguna and Cochiti have a Grab Day.

12	Santa Clara Feast Day in honor of patron St. Clara. Corn, Harvest, and Buffalo or Comanche dances are featured after mass.
15	Zia Feast Day in honor of the community's patron saint, Our Lady of the Assumption. Mass, processions, ritual clowns, and the Corn dance.
28	Spanish Fiesta at Isleta to honor San Augustin. Carnival, concessions, and mass, with no dancing. The fiesta resumes again on September 3-4.

September

2	Acoma Feast Day in honor of patron St. Stephen. The Acoma Indians return from nearby residential villages to the old mesa-top pueblo for fiesta. Mass is celebrated in the magnificent mission church. After a noisy procession, there is dancing all afternoon on the plaza, followed by speeches and a quieter procession back to the church.
4	Isleta Feast Day, continuing the ceremonies in honor of St. Augustine started on August 28. On the evening before there is a carnival, Spanish music and dancing, and later, Indian dancing and a bonfire. Feast Day begins with an early mass and procession, followed by the feast and Harvest dance.
8	Celebration of the Nativity of the Virgin Mary at San Ildefonso and Laguna. There are Harvest and social dances in Encinal Village at Laguna and a Corn dance at San Ildefonso.
Weekend after Labor Day	Fiesta de Santa Fe. The most elaborate of the Spanish fiestas, celebrating the Spanish reconquest of the city in 1692.

On Friday evening most Santa Fe residents participate in the burning of Zozobra, a 40-foot-high puppet representing Old Man Gloom, and continue festivities afterwards on the plaza. On Saturday there is a parade for children and their pets, entertainment on the plaza, an historical re-enactment of Don Diego de Vargas' re-entry of the city in 17th century costume, and a grand ball in the evening. The big event during the day on Sunday is the Hysterical/Historical parade, which is much more the former than the latter. The Fiesta concludes solemnly on Sunday evening with mass in the Cathedral and a candlelight procession from there to the Cross of the Martyrs, a hill-top memorial to the 23 Franciscan priests killed in the 1680 Pueblo Revolt. The Fiesta used to be held on Labor Day weekend, but the date was changed because the event was being overwhelmed by visitors, probably the only time that city leaders have ever tried to discourage tourism in Santa Fe.

19 Laguna Feast Day in honor of patron San Jose. After mass in the beautiful mission church there are various dances in the plaza and a big carnival.

30 Taos Feast Day in honor of patron San Geronimo. Begins on the evening before with vespers, a Sundown dance, and singing and drumming throughout the night. There is a procession the next morning after an early mass and then a ceremonial relay race. Later, ritual clowns appear, play around the village for awhile, and then start the pole climb, which ends in the retrieval of a sheep carcass and gifts from the top of a tall shaft. There is an active trade fair all day.

October

4 Nambe Feast Day in honor of patron San Francisco de Assisi. Vespers and a firelight procession are held on the evening before. On Feast Day there are various dances in the afternoon.

November

12 Jemez and Tesuque Feast Days in honor of San Diego, the patron saint of both communities. The Jemez fiesta includes mass, the Corn dance, clowns, and a trade fair. In Tesuque there is a Deer dance at dawn, then mass and a procession, followed by more dancing.

December

Early Zuni Shalako. Sometimes held in late November, the date is set a few weeks in advance. The ceremonies, which involve no Catholic rituals, last 24 hours straight, from one afternoon to the next. From midnight to dawn, 9-foot-tall Shalako figures dance in newly-built or remodeled houses, to bless the residences. At dawn the Shalakos engage in a dramatic ritual race on their stilts.

12 Pojoaque Feast Day in honor of Our Lady of Guadalupe. After mass there are Bow and Arrow, Buffalo, or Comanche dances in front of the church and later at the community center. Nambe celebrates the day with the Deer dance. Jemez performs Los Matachines, a dance introduced by the Spanish colonists which portrays the universal struggle between good and evil.

Pre-Christmas	Festive Christmas celebrations in Santa Fe and other Spanish communities. Residents decorate homes with *farolitos*, candles placed in sand inside paper bags. Some residents burn *luminarias*, or small bonfires, traditionally lighted on Christmas Eve to represent the fires of the Bethlehem shepherds. Old Christmas pageants are staged around town in Catholic churches and homes. The most common pageant is Las Posadas, a re-enactment of Mary and Joseph's quest for shelter.
24-25	Various dances in many of the pueblos on Christmas Eve and Day. The most common dances are Los Matachines and the Deer dance.

Part Three

The best places

Galleries and Shops

Artists and artisans of the Santa Fe area are producing more fine work today than at any other time in the city's long history. The current generation of Pueblo potters, Spanish woodcarvers, and art colony emigres is energetically extending and reinforcing the cultural traditions of the area. Spending time with their work in Santa Fe galleries and shops is both delightful and enlightening, as important in absorbing the city's heritage as walks along old, adobe-lined streets.

The abundance and quality of current work has stimulated a major gallery boom in Santa Fe. In the last two decades the number of shops offering original art and hand-crafted products from the area has leaped from a handful to over 150. Today there are considerably more galleries per capita in Santa Fe than in New York City. One recent visitor, the music critic of the Washington *Post*, writing a review of the Opera, claimed that there wasn't a shopping environment comparable to Santa Fe this side of Florence.

The ambiance, informality, and friendliness of the local galleries make them comfortable places for looking and learning. Even when one has no intention of buying anything, browsing is a very pleasant experience.

The only difficulty with enjoying the galleries is deciding where to go. Their recent proliferation and frequent changes pose challenges even for long-time residents. The following directory is a comprehensive listing of galleries and shops which carry some selection of work from the area, with quality ratings and brief descriptions of what they offer. All types of handmade work are covered, including clothing and furniture.

The shops are listed under the general categories of Indian Art and Crafts; Hispanic Art and Crafts; Paintings, Prints, and Sculpture; and Contemporary Southwestern Crafts. The Hispanic category includes some places which carry only imported work—the one exception to the criterion of representing area artists and artisans—because they handle handcrafted items which reflect indigenous styles.

Galleries and shops which carry work from more than one of the general categories are listed only once, in the field of their strongest selection. Their other offerings are noted in the descriptions. Anyone looking for a particular type of item should check the descriptions in each of the categories to identify all of the appropriate places to try. The best galleries often have outstanding selections in secondary fields.

The rating system involves four classifications:

**** A four-star rating designates a museum quality gallery, worth browsing for educational purposes at any time. Generally they are expensive.

*** A three-star rating indicates excellence and depth in the selection. Most of these places are expensive, but not always.

** Two-star galleries and shops carry some work of high quality from the area, either a few fine pieces included with items from outside of the Southwest, or a range of local craftsmanship that varies in skill and price. It is important to note that many places receive this rating only because their selection of regional work is limited. In cases where the description indicates a "small selection" of items from the area included with products from elsewhere, the rating is based on the range of local choices and does not reflect any deficiencies in quality; these shops all carry some fine Southwestern work and many of them have an excellent overall selection.

* One-star shops are good places to look for moderately-priced items.

People who are unfamiliar with the unique artistic traditions and crafts of the area should consult Part One, or other appropriate materials, before going browsing or shopping. It can be difficult otherwise to understand the values embodied in the work. The earlier chapters provide a basic orientation to the Indian, Spanish, and Anglo cultural traditions of the area, and mention some of the prominent artists in each.

Indian arts and crafts

** Blue Gem of La Fonda. 100 E. San Francisco, in La Fonda Hotel. Wide range of modern work, plus some local Hispanic crafts.

** Bovis Gallery of Primitive Art. 213 Galisteo. Small selection of historic Southwestern pieces included with fine primitive art from around the world.

**** Case Trading Post. 704 Camino Lejo, in the Wheelwright Museum of the American Indian. Some historic pieces and a wide range of modern work.

*** Cristof's. 106 W. San Francisco. Specializes in kachina dolls, weavings, sandpaintings, and bead jewelry.

* Desert Son. 725 Canyon. Some jewelry included with leather moccasins and accessories.

**** Dewey-Kofron Gallery. 74 E. San Francisco, on the plaza. Fine selection of modern work and some historic pieces, plus Western paintings and sculpture, and occasional Hispanic antiques.

* Don Juan's Gifts. 30 Sena Plaza. Mainly jewelry with a small selection of Hispanic work.

* Dressman's Gifts. 54 Lincoln, on the plaza. Jewelry and gifts.

*** W.S. Dutton's Rare Things. 138 Sena Plaza. Specializes in historic pottery, old-style kachina dolls, jewelry, and Hispanic religious art.

* E & B Buffalo Trading. 227 Don Gaspar, in Santa Fe Village. Mainly jewelry.

** The Eagle Dancer Southwest. 215 E. De Vargas, in the "Oldest House." Wide range of modern work.

** Gallery of the Old West. 201 W. San Francisco, in the "Original Trading Post." Small selection of historic pieces included with other artifacts from the old West.

** Holbrook Gallery. 402 Old Santa Fe Trail. Small selection of historic Southwestern pieces included with a fine range of crafts and artifacts from ancient civilizations.

*** Indian Trader West. 208 W. San Francisco. Wide range of modern work and some historic pieces.

** Kachina House and Gallery. 236 Delgado. Fine selection of kachina dolls plus some other modern work.

*** Kiva Shop. 57 Old Santa Fe Trail, on the plaza. Wide range and large selection of modern work.

*** Mudd-Carr Gallery. 338 E. De Vargas. Historic and modern pottery and weavings, plus a strong selection of traditional Hispanic art, some from New Mexico.

** Robert F. Nichols. 652 Canyon. Small selection of historic Southwestern pieces included with a fine collection of American country antiques and folk art.

** Ortega's Turquoise Mesa. 101 W. San Francisco, on the plaza. Wide range of modern work.

*** Packard's Indian Trading Company. 61 Old Santa Fe Trail, on the plaza. Wide range and large selection of modern work, plus a small selection of local Hispanic crafts.

** Palace of the Governors Museum Shop. In the Palace of the Governors, on the plaza. Mainly pottery and jewelry, plus a small selection of local Hispanic crafts.

* Frank Patania's. 119 E. Palace. Mainly jewelry with some other modern work.

** Quintana's. 113 E. San Francisco. Wide range of modern work.

** Quivira Shop. 114 Old Santa Fe Trail. Nice pottery plus a small selection of other work.

** James Reid, Ltd. 112 E. Palace. Small selection of jewelry included with fine antique silver pieces and coins.

* Ruybalid's. 113 and 117 E. Palace. Jewelry and some Hispanic and contemporary crafts.

**** Santa Fe East. 200 Old Santa Fe Trail. Primarily fine jewelry with some pottery, plus paintings and prints.

** Santa Fe Gallery. 422 Old Santa Fe Trail. Small selection of historic Southwestern pieces included with a fine collection of crafts and artifacts from ancient civilizations.

* Santa Fe Indian Rugs. 227 Don Gaspar, in Santa Fe Village. Navajo weavings, plus a small selection of Mexican rugs.

* Silver Sun. 656 Canyon. Mainly jewelry with some other modern work, plus a small

selection of local contemporary crafts.

** Streets of Taos. 200 Canyon. Range of old and recent work plus some Hispanic carvings and locally-made clothes.

* Sun Country Traders. 123 E. Water. Mainly jewelry and pottery.

** Susan's Christmas Shop. 115 E. Palace. Small selection of pottery items included with Christmas decorations from around the world.

* Turquoise Tipi. 227 Don Gaspar, in Santa Fe Village. Mainly jewelry with some other modern work.

** Unicorn Antiques. 314 Guadalupe. Small selection of old jewelry included with antiques.

Hispanic arts and crafts

*** Jeffrey Adams Antiques. 602 Canyon. Spanish colonial antiques and religious art.

* All the World's Children. 112 Old Santa Fe Trail. Small selection of Central and South American clothes and crafts included with other imports.

** Architectural Antiques. 812 Canyon. Spanish colonial doors, fixtures, and other architectural detail.

*** Artesanos Imports. 222 Galisteo. Fine Mexican crafts and furnishings.

* Ayocuan. 137 W. San Francisco. Indian rugs from Central and South America, plus some local contemporary crafts.

*** Claiborne Gallery. 701 Canyon. Spanish colonial antiques and religious art, plus some historic Indian pottery.

*** Culpepper Gallery. 129 W. San Francisco. Central and South American paintings and crafts, mainly from the colonial period.

** Doodlet's. 120 Don Gaspar. Small selection of Hispanic crafts included with a diverse array of gifts and treats.

*El Sombrero. 211 Old Santa Fe Trail, in the Inn at Loretto. Mexican imports.

** El Telar. 102 E. Water, in El Centro Mall. Wide range of imported crafts, mainly from Mexico, and some local Hispanic and Indian work.

*** El Trastero. 125 Sena Plaza. Nice range of modern, local work.

*** The Gamut. 54 E. San Francisco. Central and South American clothes for women and some local and imported Hispanic crafts included with fine items from around the world. Also prints and contemporary crafts.

** Gordon Galleries. 409 Canyon. Southwestern antiques included with paintings and prints from around the world.

** Habitat. 222 Shelby. Small selection of Spanish colonial antiques included with other furnishings.

* Haitian Art Gallery. 301 E. Alameda. Paintings, sculpture, and artifacts from Haiti.

* Harvest. 558 Canyon. Central and South American clothing included with other imported wear.

* House and Table. 20 Sena Plaza. Some Hispanic and contemporary crafts included with other decorative and utilitarian items for the home.

* The Hughes House. 118 Old Santa Fe Trail. Indian rugs from Central and South America, some local *santos*, and Pueblo pottery.

** La Bodega. 667 Canyon. Central and South

American crafts, antiques, and clothing, plus Indian jewelry and pottery.

** La Espuela Antiques. 156 E. De Vargas. Spanish colonial antiques and other old items.

*** La Mariquita. 104 W. San Francisco. Fine Mexican clothing for women.

** Life-Style Santa Fe. 211 Old Santa Fe Trail, in the Inn at Loretto. Spanish colonial reproductions and custom-made furniture.

*** Little Plaza Gallery. 125 E. Palace. Paintings and prints by prominent Mexican artists.

* Lujan's Place. 218 Galisteo. Mexican kitchen ware, plus an interesting assortment of herbs and spices.

** Don J. Madtson Antiques. 806 Old Santa Fe Trail. Combination of Spanish American, British, and U.S. antiques.

*** Davis Mather Gallery of Regional Folk Art. 141 Lincoln. Local and Mexican woodcarvings.

** Old Mexico Shop. 141 W. Water. Large selection of Mexican crafts, furnishings, and clothes.

** Ben Ortega's Studio. Bishop's Lodge Road in Tesuque. *Santos.*

*** Ortega's Weaving Shop. Chimayo. The largest selection of Rio Grande weavings in the area.

** Santa Fe Company. 419 Canyon. Local carvings and imported crafts and furnishings.

*** Santa Fe Store. 211 Old Santa Fe Trail, behind the Inn at Loretto. Local carvings and imported clothes and crafts, mainly from Mexico.

** The Shop. 227 Don Gaspar, in Santa Fe Village. Small selection of Spanish American pieces among other antiques and furnishings.

** Shop of the Frightened Owl. 1117 Canyon. Spanish colonial furnishings.

* South American Arts and Crafts Gallery. 115 Old Santa Fe Trail, in La Fonda Hotel. South American crafts.

*** Southwest Spanish Craftsmen. 922 Canyon. Spanish colonial antiques and reproductions.

* Tesoros de Espana. 227 Don Gaspar, in Santa Fe Village. Imports from Spain.

** Three Centuries Gallery. 727 Canyon. Small selection of colonial furnishings included with other antiques and collectibles.

* Voice of the Turtle Gallery. 317 Guadalupe. Some Central and South American clothes included with incense and books.

Paintings, prints, and sculpture

** An American Place. 725 Canyon. Contemporary prints and posters.

* Art Center. 102 E. Water, in El Centro Mall. Representational work.

** Artists' Gallery. 125 W. Palace. Contemporary paintings, prints, and local crafts.

* Howard Bobb's Gallery. 113 E. San Francisco. Western art.

**** Marilyn Butler Fine Art. 112 W. San Francisco. Contemporary work.

*** Canyon Road Art Gallery. 710 Canyon. Representational work and some local Spanish carvings.

**** Linda Durham Gallery. 400 Canyon. Contemporary paintings, prints, and sculpture.

** Eason Gallery. 149 E. Alameda. Contemporary work, mainly from outside the Southwest.

*** Enthios Gallery. 1111 Paseo de Peralta and in the Inn at Loretto. The rating is for the larger gallery on Paseo de Peralta, which carries contemporary paintings, prints, and sculpture.

* Father Sky-Mother Earth Gallery. 227 Don Gaspar, in Santa Fe Village. Contemporary work.

**** Fenn Galleries. 1075 Paseo de Peralta. The Founders and their tradition, plus fine Indian and Hispanic work and more.

* Field Contemporary. 110 Old Santa Fe Trail. Contemporary work.

* Gallery Americana. 102 E. Water, in El Centro Mall. Western art.

* Gallery of the 21st Century. 102 E. Water, in El Centro Mall. Primarily posters of contemporary Indian work.

*** The Gallery Wall. 104 Old Santa Fe Trail. Contemporary paintings, prints, and sculpture by Indian artists.

** Gondeck Gallery. 211 Old Santa Fe Trail, behind the Inn at Loretto. Prints by contemporary Indian artists.

** Graphics House Gallery. 702 Canyon. Contemporary prints.

** Hand Graphics. 418 Montezuma, near Guadalupe. Contemporary prints.

**** Heydt/Bair Gallery. 376 Garcia. Contemporary paintings, prints, photographs, and sculpture.

**** Elaine Horwitch Gallery. 129 W. Palace. Contemporary paintings and prints, plus local Hispanic folk art.

*** Jamison Galleries. 111 E. San Francisco. Representational work.

** Janus Gallery. 110 Galisteo. Contemporary work.

** Bob Kapoun Vintage Photograph Gallery. 57 Old Santa Fe Trail, on the plaza. Old Southwestern photography.

** Lippincott Studio/Gallery. 1270 Canyon. Contemporary work.

*** Los Llanos Gallery. 72 E. San Francisco. Contemporary work.

** Ernesto Mayans. 601 Canyon. Contemporary work.

*** Linda McAdoo Galleries. 503 Canyon. Some of the Founders and other work in their tradition.

*** The Munson Gallery. 653 Canyon. Primarily representational work, plus the Ann Thomas collection of Pueblo pottery.

*** O'Meara Gallery. 130 W. Palace. The Founders and other work in their tradition.

** Bob Parks Gallery. 102 E. Water in El Centro Mall. Western art.

* Pelham Galleries. 101 Washington. Primarily representational work.

*** Gerald P. Peters. 439 Camino del Monte Sol. Paintings by the Founders and contemporary sculpture.

** C. G. Rein. 122 W. San Francisco. Contemporary work.

* Roger H. Rodgers Studio of the Arts. 1136 Canyon. Collages, paintings, and crafts.

*** S. Rudy Gallery. 616D Paseo de la Loma. Contemporary paintings, prints, photographs, and sculpture.

*** Santa Fe Gallery of Photography. 102 W. San Francisco. Photography.

* Savage Galleries. 102 E. Water. Western art.

* Scharf Gallery. 76 E. San Francisco. Representational and contemporary work.

**** Shidoni Sculpture Gallery. Bishop's Lodge Road in Tesuque. Wide range of sculpture from western bronzes to contemporary pieces.

** Shop of the Rainbow Man. 107 E. Palace. Representational paintings included with crystal, brass, and china pieces, and some Indian work.

** Agnes Sims. 600 Canyon. Primitive-style paintings and sculpture.

* V. Stiha Gallery. La Fonda Hotel. Western art.

* Bill Tate Gallery. 713 Canyon. Unusual paintings by the unusual proprietor.

** Carol Thornton Gallery. 211 Old Santa Fe Trail, in the Inn at Loretto. Contemporary and western work.

** The Triumvirate. 707 Canyon. Contemporary work.

** Wadle Galleries. 123 W. Palace. Primarily representational work.

** Dell Weston Bronze Sculpture. 1310 Siler. Western and contemporary work.

*** The White Hyacinth. 137 W. San Francisco. Best poster gallery in town.

** Williams Gallery. 201 W. San Francisco, in the "Original Trading Post." Western art and some historic Indian pieces.

*** Woodrow Wilson Fine Arts. 102 E. Water, in El Centro Mall. Some of the Founders and other work in their tradition.

Contemporary southwestern crafts

* Edda Lynne Allen Studio/Gallery. 727 Canyon. Functional stoneware and other crafts.

* Aquarius Glass Co. 656 Canyon. Stained glass.

*** Arachne Fiberarts. 217 W. San Francisco. Handwoven clothing and weaving supplies.

*** Arius Tile Co. 114 Don Gaspar. Wide selection of ceramic tiles.

** Christina Bergh Handweaving. 924 Paseo de Peralta. Handwoven tapestries and home accessories.

** Bird Watcher Shop. 716 Canyon. Some locally-made clothes included with other casual women's wear.

** Bloomers 'n' Britches. 235 Don Gaspar, in Springer Plaza. Handmade children's clothing.

* Brass Shop. 118 Old Santa Fe Trail. Some local work included with other brass items.

** Canyon Leatherworks. 656 Canyon. Leather clothing, belts, and hats.

** Ceramic Galleries of Santa Fe. 108 Galisteo. Ceramic tiles.

** Ciel d' Or Gallery. 235 Don Gaspar, in Springer Plaza. Jewelry, blown glass, paintings, and sculpture.

**** The Contemporary Craftsman. 112 Don Gaspar. The best general crafts gallery in Santa Fe. Wide range and large selection of work.

* Crystal Reflections. 118 Old Santa Fe Trail. Jewelry, gems, and mineral specimens.

** De la Harpe Carved Doors and Furniture. 707 Canyon. Contemporary and traditional designs.

* Del Sol. Old Santa Fe Trail at Water, in La Fonda Hotel. Decorative and functional crafts.

** Dell Woodworks. 401 Rodeo. Rustic "Taos-style" furniture, shown at Nambe Mills shop, 301 E. Alameda.

* Fickery. 720 Canyon. Functional stoneware.

* Galeria Miguel. 616 Canyon. Handmade women's clothing and accessories.

* Glorianna's Fine Crafts. 55 W. Marcy. Some jewelry included with beads and other crafts supplies.

*** Golden Bough. 211 Old Santa Fe Trail, in the Inn at Loretto. Contemporary gold jewelry.

** Golden Web. 102 E. Water, in El Centro Mall. Contemporary jewelry.

** Gusterman's. 126 E. Palace. Silver jewelry primarily.

* Gypsy-Van Buren Gallery. 706 Canyon. Handmade clothing along with prints and other items.

* The Hand Maiden. 102 E. Water, in El Centro Mall. Functional crafts, mainly pottery.

** Handwoven Originals. 211 Old Santa Fe Trail, in the Inn at Loretto. Handwoven clothing and accessories.

** House of the Mountain Mouse. 927 Paseo de Peralta. Some locally-made miniatures included with doll houses and accessories.

*** Jett. 644 Canyon. Contemporary jewelry.

** Judy's Unique Apparel. 714 Canyon. Some locally-made clothes included with other casual women's wear.

** Kailer-Grant Designs. 143 Lincoln. Small selection of local and imported crafts, and some paintings, included with fine home furnishings.

* Las Cosas Gift and Card Shop. 55 Old Santa Fe Trail, on the plaza. Small selection of local work included with gifts and cards.

* Leather Gallery. 108 Old Santa Fe Trail. Leather accessories and some jewelry.

* Lee-Tzu Boutique. 727 Canyon. Handmade women's clothing along with imported wear.

** Ross LewAllen Jewelry. 109 Washington. Contemporary jewelry, including the popular "Ear-cuff."

* The Light Merchant. 109 Washington. Stained glass.

** L'Isle Designs. 300 Garcia. Handwoven clothing and weaving supplies.

** Lujo Furniture Craftsmen. 631 Old Santa Fe Trail. Custom-made wood furniture in any style.

* Marco Polo Shop. 132 E. Palace. Small selection of local work included with gifts and clothes.

** Marcy Street Card Shop. 85 W. Marcy. Cards designed by local artists, among others, and some jewelry.

** The Market. 111 E. Palace. Handwoven fashions and pottery.

** Dennis McMillan's Woodworks. 340 Read, at the corner of Guadalupe. Heavy pine furniture, "Taos-style."

** Melting Point Glass Works and Pottery. 821 Canyon. Pottery and glass, with an open studio.

*** Nambe Mills. 301 E. Alameda. Distinctive metal cooking and serving ware. Would rate four-star if the showroom sold the best work instead of seconds mainly.

** Origins. 135 W. San Francisco. Small selection of locally-made clothes included with a delightful range of imported women's wear and accessories.

*** Overland Sheepskin Co. 214 Galisteo. Sheepskin coats, vests, and accessories for men and women, made in Taos.

** Quilts by Lily. 435 Guadalupe. Quilts in contemporary designs.

** Ralph and Joyce. 129 W. San Francisco. Pottery and weaving.

* Rio Grande Tiles. 102 E. Water, in El Centro Mall. Ceramic tiles along with some Indian and imported crafts.

** Rio Madera Woodworks. La Cienega. Heavy pine furniture, "Taos-style." Lack of a showroom allows them to offer bargain prices for this distinctive style of work.

*** Running Ridge Gallery. 640 Canyon. Wide range of fine crafts plus prints.

** Salamander Leathers. 78 and 100 E. San Francisco. Small selection of locally-made clothes included with a fine range of fashionable western leather wear for men and women.

* The Sandman. 137 W. San Francisco. Some locally-made items included with a range of bedding products.

** Santa Fe Footwear. 435 Guadalupe. Handcrafted soft-leather boots and shoes.

* Santa Fe Pottery. 323 Guadalupe. Functional pottery.

*** Santa Fe Weaving Center. 124 Galisteo and 821 Canyon. Women's clothing and other handwoven items with weaving supplies.

*** Selective Eye. 118 Don Gaspar. Contemporary gold jewelry.

** Something Fine. 435 Guadalupe. Some locally-made clothes included with other casual women's wear.

** Sunrise of Santa Fe. 111 Old Santa Fe Trail, in La Fonda Hotel. Contemporary jewelry.

** Territorial Tiles of Santa Fe. 103 W. San Francisco. Ceramic tiles.

* Tidbits. 300 Garcia. Small selection of handmade clothing included with gifts.

* Touch of Love Gallery. 109 Old Santa Fe Trail, in La Fonda Hotel. Jewelry and wood sculpture.

* Touch of Trim. 129 W. San Francisco. Clothing, accessories, and other fabrics.

** Two Fourteen. 214 Old Santa Fe Trail. Small selection of locally-made clothes and accessories included with other women's fashions.

* Virginia Trading Post. 82 E. San Francisco, on the plaza. Small selection of local crafts included with imports and gifts.

** Wild West Clothing. 435 Guadalupe. Handmade western clothes for men and women.

** Zephyr. 138 Sena Plaza. Local designer clothing for women.

Restaurants

The native New Mexican food of Santa Fe, served in half of the local restaurants, is a piquant expression of the city's living heritage. Santa Fe's long isolation from the rest of Hispanic America produced a distinctive style of local cooking, simple in ingredients but wonderfully spicy. The native food differs from any of the regional cuisines of Mexico, from "Tex-Mex" cooking, and certainly from the flavorless fare served as Mexican food in the East. What the restaurants of Santa Fe lack in variety, compared to large cities at least, they recoup in intensity and authenticity.

The primary ingredient of New Mexican cooking is the chile pepper, which is actually more closely related to the tomato plant than to the shrub which produces black pepper. Native to tropical America, chile has been grown under irrigation in New Mexico for at least 400 years. When harvested the chile pods are generally green and are used in that form, chopped in small pieces, in some dishes. Or the pods can be dried, which turns them red, and then ground to make another style of sauce. Many dishes served in Santa Fe restaurants can be made with either green or red chile, depending on the preference of the customer. Either version can be hot or mild, varying with the particular chiles used, but neither will be bland.

The other basic ingredients of New Mexican meals are tortillas, pinto beans, *posole*, and *sopaipillas*. Tortillas and beans are common in all forms of Mexican cooking, but are prepared somewhat differently in New Mexico. The beans are seldom refried, which is the most typical treatment elsewhere, and the tortillas are frequently made from a special blue corn meal that is rarely found outside the area. *Posole*, a type of hominy cooked with chile and pork, is usually served instead of Spanish rice. *Sopaipillas* are a form of fried bread, often eaten with the entree, covered with honey. Cheese, chicken, pork, or beef are included in most meals in some fashion, but normally are a secondary flavor.

Even the best New Mexican cooking in Santa Fe is fairly inexpensive. It's difficult to spend more than $8 a person on a meal, including drinks and dessert, and easy to be satisfied for $5 or less. Long waiting lines, frequently encountered in the summer, are the only reasonable excuse for not having the native food at least once a day.

There are alternatives, however, and some that are very special. The best restaurants featuring other cuisines — ranging from American to Japanese to French — are described and rated below under the category of "other local favorites," separate from the New Mexican restaurants.

The rating system is based strictly on the quality of preparation and ingredients relative to other restaurants offering similar food in the United States. The ratings try to exclude bias for one kind of cuisine over another by comparing local restaurants to ones with analogous menus in other cities. Places which feature continental food, for example, do not have an inherent advantage in the ratings, as they seem to in many systems, just because of what they print on the menu. If a restaurant excels with complex dishes it gains an advantage over a place offering good, simpler fare, but the test is preparation, not pretension.

Though the ratings are based on the quality of the food, they also generally reflect atmosphere and service fairly well. The top-rated restaurants usually have a charming, traditional Santa Fe atmosphere and some of the best service in the city, though the service tends to be informal everywhere. There are, however, several New Mexican restaurants which serve excellent food in a plain setting and even more one-star restaurants among the "other local favorites" which provide wonderful atmosphere. The descriptions indicate what to expect.

There are four categories in the ratings:

**** A four-star restaurant is one of the best in the country for its style of cooking.

*** Three-star restaurants are consistently excellent.

** Two stars mean excellence in many of the choices much of the time.

* One star indicates a good place to have the kind of food offered, a restaurant which would be competitive in its class in any city.

A recent change in the law now allows restaurants to serve beer and wine without a full liquor license and almost all do. The wine lists are generally limited, but the selection of good imported Mexican beer is much better than in most parts of the country. Restaurants which also serve cocktails are noted.

In the descriptions, "expensive" refers to entrees over $10. "Inexpensive" means less than $5, and "moderate" falls in between.

New Mexican restaurants

** Cordelia's No. 2. 1348 Pacheco.

Eating at Cordelia's is like going to a friend's home. The restaurant is located in a converted house in a residential neighborhood, with dining in a backyard patio as well as inside. The home-cooked food is simple and tasty, and the service is as warm as the chile. The menu includes sandwiches and American entrees in addition to traditional New Mexican items.

Lunch and dinner. Closed Sunday. Cocktails. Reservations accepted. Inexpensive. No credit cards.

*** Dave's. 1215 Hickox.

Dave's took over Tomasita's old location when the latter moved downtown, and managed to maintain the local popularity of the spot as a neighborhood cafe. The New Mexican food is very good and plentiful, the hamburgers enormous, and the desserts worth the calories. The restaurant is small and friendly, and so are the checks. It's a wonder that anyone can cook so well in such a tiny kitchen, situated right in the dining area, but Dave does it without faltering.

Lunch and dinner. Closed Sunday. No cocktails. No reservations. Inexpensive. No credit cards.

* Don Jose. 102 Airport Road.

Located on the south edge of town, at the intersection of Cerrillos and Airport Roads, Don Jose is the best of the highway cafes in the area. The atmosphere inside is comfortable and family-oriented. The food, which includes a few American items among the regional specialties, is honest fare and the servings are large.

Lunch and dinner. Open daily. Cocktails. No reservations required. Moderately priced. Master Card and VISA accepted.

* Estrada Room. 504 W. Cordova.

There are not many decent restaurants in the country attached to a bowling alley, but the

Estrada Room is one. The food doesn't roll one over, but it is good, basic New Mexican cooking, plus steaks, sandwiches, and luncheon specials. A combined bar and restaurant, there is often live music and some limited food service after 10 p.m., both rare in Santa Fe.

Lunch and dinner. Open daily. Cocktails. Reservations accepted for large parties. Inexpensive to moderate. Master Card and VISA accepted.

* Green Onion. 1851 St. Michael's Drive.

The bar, which adjoins the restaurant, is loud and friendly, particularly on St. Patrick's Day and when the giant television screen is tuned to sports events. The restaurant is more subdued, but tends to share in the enthusiasm and noise of the bar. The menu ranges widely, but the best dishes involve the zesty chile.

Lunch and dinner. Closed Sunday. Cocktails. No reservations. Inexpensive to moderate. Master Card and VISA accepted.

** Guadalupe Cafe. 313 Guadalupe.

One of the few restaurants in town which serves breakfast, lunch, and dinner, the Guadalupe Cafe is usually excellent for any of the three. The breakfast selection includes a variety of egg and pancake dishes, served with hash browns and homemade bread. Two of the best choices are the *migas* — scrambled eggs with chile, cheese, onion, and tortilla chips — and the burrito *desayuno* — a cheese omelet wrapped in a flour tortilla and served with chile.

The lunch and dinner menus are varied, featuring several New Mexican plates, but also hamburgers, a daily Italian special, and other items. Desserts include a rich adobe pie. The restaurant is popular and often packed at dinner.

Breakfast, lunch, and dinner. Closed Saturday and Sunday. No cocktails. No reservations. Inexpensive to moderate. Master Card and VISA accepted.

** Jimmy's-Tiny's Lounge and Restaurant. Cerrillos and St. Francis.

Jimmy's-Tiny's is a neighborhood bar-cafe which resembles similar institutions in other cities. The decor is as familiar as the patrons are with each other. The menu features chicken *flautas* and enchiladas. The combination dinner is as much Texan in its style of cooking as New Mexican, but is good. A fun and popular spot.

Lunch and dinner. Closed Sunday. Cocktails. Reservations taken. Moderately priced. Master Card and VISA accepted.

*** Josie's Casa De Comida. 95 West Marcy.

Josie's is a terrific luncheon cafe, a small, inexpensive, plain downtown favorite of people working nearby. The chile *rellenos*, enchiladas, and other regional dishes are delicious, and the more standard American lunches are above average. Thankfully, the portions are not overwhelming because the desserts — listed on the blackboard and on paper notes taped to the walls — are wonderful.

The waiting area, where one is likely to be detained, is Marcy Street. Locals will line up and wait patiently on the street for a table even in the middle of winter.

Lunch only. Closed Saturday and Sunday. No cocktails. No reservations. Inexpensive. No credit cards.

* La Cocina. 1201 Cerrillos Road.

La Cocina is one of the few places in town that offers a choice between a mild or hot chile sauce, both of which match their labels. The spacious dining room is pleasantly decorated and the service is cordial. In addition to a range of New Mexican dishes, La Cocina also serves barbecued ribs, an unusual option for Santa Fe.

Lunch and dinner. Open daily. Reservations taken. No cocktails. Moderately priced. Master Card and VISA accepted.

*** La Tertulia. 416 Agua Fria.

This converted convent, now divided into several small dining rooms, used to serve the Santuario de Guadalupe across the street. The mood in the rambling old adobe is pure Santa Fe.

Both the lunch and dinner menus offer a variety of New Mexican dishes, which tend to be mild but flavorful. At lunch there are also omelets, salads, and sandwiches. In the evening steaks are served, including one smothered in green chile and one served with two *rellenos*. The homemade sangria wine, available by the pitcher, is excellent.

The service is friendly, but is sometimes flawed by an eagerness to accommodate as many people as possible. At peak periods reservations seem to be scheduled on a tight timetable.

Lunch and dinner. Closed Monday. Cocktails. Reservations advised. Moderately priced. Master Card and VISA accepted.

** Maria Ysabel. 1130 Agua Fria.

This small neighborhood restaurant has the best family-style dinner in town, served for groups of four or more. The courses include soup, appetizer, two kinds of enchiladas, *carne adovada*, and delicious *capirotada*, or Mexican bread pudding, for dessert. The same dishes are also available in individual servings, along with other specialties, though they tend to be relatively expensive in that form. On weekends there is live Spanish guitar music.

Breakfast, lunch, and dinner. Closed Sunday. No cocktails. No reservations. Inexpensive for breakfast, moderate to expensive for other meals. Master Card and VISA accepted.

* Maria's Mexican Kitchen. 555 W. Cordova.

A small family restaurant, with casual atmosphere and service, Maria's serves good, basic New Mexican food and moderately-priced steaks. The native food, simple and authentic, is a bargain.

Dinner only. Open daily. Cocktails. No reservations. Inexpensive to moderate. Master Card accepted.

** Molly's Kitchen. 530 Cerrillos Road.

The flocked wallpaper is jarring at first, but somehow begins to blend in with the exuberance of the service and the food before the end of the meal. Often the restaurant is more spirited and noisy than the attached lounge.

The New Mexican dishes are tasty and plentiful, flavored to attract a local clientele. Sandwiches are also offered.

Lunch and dinner. Closed Sunday. Cocktails. Reservations taken. Inexpensive to moderate. Master Card and VISA accepted.

**** Rancho de Chimayo.

Located about 25 miles north of Santa Fe in the village of Chimayo, the restaurant is in an old adobe *hacienda* that was the ancestral home of the owner, Arturo Jaramillo. The drive from town is beautiful, particularly at sunset, and the ambiance in the *hacienda* is grand but comfortable. In the summer one can dine outside on the patio, and in the winter move inside to one of the cozy, small rooms with a fireplace.

The food is very traditional. The local favorite is *carne adovada,* a pork chop cooked in hot red chile, which can be ordered as an entree, or with a combination plate, or in a burrito. A milder choice is the *sopaipilla relleno,* a large *sopaipilla* stuffed with meat, beans, and chile and covered with chile and cheese. The *flan,* or creme caramel, is an excellent dessert. The bar serves good margaritas and a specialty called the Chimayo Cocktail, a nice combination of tequila and apple juice.

Lunch and dinner. Open daily. Reservations advised. Moderately priced. Master Card and VISA accepted.

* Rincon del Oso. 639 Old Santa Fe Trail.

South of downtown, a few blocks from the Capitol, the Rincon del Oso attracts a good luncheon crowd from state offices. The restaurant's relatively mild native food is well prepared and the service is genial. The atmosphere is agreeable and relaxing, accentuated by paintings, plants, and local Spanish crafts.

Lunch only. Closed Saturday and Sunday. No cocktails. No reservations. Inexpensive. No credit cards.

**** The Shed. 113½ Palace.

The most popular place for lunch in Santa Fe is The Shed. There is usually a line after 11:30, but the wait is pleasant in the front courtyard, originally the central patio of a large *hacienda*.

The enchiladas with blue corn tortillas are the best in town and the other New Mexican dishes are also top quality. The *posole* and beans served with several of the lunches are superb. The hamburger with green chile and cheese is less traditional, but full of local flavor.

Daily soups and desserts are listed on a blackboard in each of the charming dining rooms. The green chile soup with potatoes is an excellent starter on a cold day. The mocha cake is rich and heavy and the lemon souffle is light and delicate.

Lunch only. Closed Sunday. No reservations. No cocktails. Inexpensive. No credit cards.

*** Tecolote. 1203 Cerrillos Road.

Despite the inauspicious location, Tecolote serves the best breakfast in town, complete with a basket of homemade biscuits and blueberry muffins. This is one American restaurant which knows how to make omelets. The Santa Fe Omelet — filled with green chile and cheese — is terrific and certain to open your eyes wide. The *huevos rancheros* are also splendid, and the orange juice is freshly squeezed.

Breakfast and lunch. Closed Tuesday. No cocktails. No reservations. Inexpensive. No credit cards.

** Tia Sophia's. 125 W. San Francisco.

A typical Western American downtown cafe in appearance, Tia Sophia's fulfills the expectation with straight-forward local cooking for an honest price. The breakfast menu includes the standards, both regional and national, and the breakfast burrito — hash browns and bacon wrapped in a flour tortilla and served with chile. There is a daily luncheon special, which is always tasty and filling, in addition to the usual New Mexican options.

Breakfast and lunch. Closed Sunday. No cocktails. No reservations. Inexpensive. Master Card and VISA accepted.

*** Tomasita's. 500 Guadalupe.

Tomasita's started as a neighborhood restaurant, serving authentic local food to a local clientele in sparse surroundings. When the restaurant moved into the central area of town in recent years, expanded, obtained a liquor license, and became uptown in decor, many locals feared that the flavor would be lost. So far, however, the food has not been affected by the move and the prices have remained extraordinarily low.

The Mexican and the combination plates, which are very similar, are both good choices. The portions are large in these and other dishes and the service is fast and friendly, once you are seated. Unless you arrive early, the wait for a table can easily be as long as the dinner.

Lunch and dinner. Closed Sunday and Monday. Cocktails. No reservations. Inexpensive. No credit cards.

Other local favorites

* The Bull Ring. 414 Old Santa Fe Trail.

Located next to the state Capitol, The Bull Ring is popular with legislators and other state officials. The large bar can be a noisy distraction during legislative sessions, but otherwise the setting is as relaxing as it is attractive, and the service is cordial. The menu ranges broadly in selection, from American to continental to New Mexican, and the dishes vary as widely in the freshness of ingredients. When the quality of the food matches the atmosphere and service, which is fairly often, The Bull Ring is a delight.

Lunch and dinner. Closed Sunday. Cocktails.

Reservations advised. Moderate to expensive. American Express, Carte Blanche, Master Card, and VISA accepted.

* Chez Edouard. 239 Johnson Street.

Pleasantly designed and thorough in service, Chez Edouard has potential, but is too new to have been tested by time. The French chef-owner offers daily specials, often seafood, and a regular menu which includes chicken, veal, steak, pork, and trout.

Lunch and dinner. Closed Monday. No cocktails. Reservations advised. Moderate to expensive. Master Card and VISA accepted.

** The Compound. 653 Canyon Road.

The best-known restaurant in Santa Fe, winner of several national awards, is no longer consistent in its ability to serve an excellent meal on every occasion. The food is usually very good, however, and The Compound remains a wonderful dining environment.

Designer Alexander Girard did a magnificent job in converting a 19th century *hacienda* into an intimate and sensuous restaurant. Inside the style is distinctively Santa Fe, but the attention to detail reaches well beyond the normal informality of local design. The walled garden outside, full of old-world character, is a fine spot to eat in the summer.

The continental menu includes a variety of meat and fresh fish entrees. The daily special is usually a good choice. The wine list is one of the best in town.

Lunch and dinner. Closed Monday. Cocktails. Reservations required. Moderate to expensive. American Express accepted.

** El Farol. 802 Canyon Road.

The plain, worn exterior of El Farol's old adobe conceals one of the most romantic dining spaces in the city. The furnishings are certainly not grand, but the total effect is just right for a small, casual bistro in Santa Fe. The bar, a couple of doors up the street, is decorated differently, in old wood and stained glass, but is equally cozy.

The menu is limited and some of the entrees are routine. The best bet is the shrimp stuffed with crab. The entree salad is good and the enchiladas are fine if you like them mild.

Dinner only. Closed Sunday and Monday. Cocktails. No reservations. Moderately priced. No credit cards.

** Ernie's. 731 Canyon Road.

The main dining room, an enclosed courtyard with a fountain and trees, is an enticing spot to eat. The food is well prepared and some of the dishes are first rate. The *pate maison* is a superb appetizer, and the daily specials and desserts can be comparable in quality. Most of the regular menu items, mainly meat, are above average, but unlikely to make anyone splash around in the fountain.

Lunch and dinner. Closed Sunday. Cocktails. Reservations advised. Moderate to expensive. Master Card and VISA accepted.

* The French Pastry Shop. La Fonda Hotel.

The French Pastry Shop is normally packed all day with people having breakfast, lunch, or just coffee and conversation. The buttery croissants are sumptuous and the other rich pastries are almost as good. Additional possibilities include crepes, sandwiches, and quiches.

Breakfast and lunch. Closed Wednesday. No cocktails. No reservations. Inexpensive. No credit cards.

*** Santa Fe Gourmet. 72 West Marcy.

The Gourmet is the best place for a soup and sandwich lunch in Santa Fe. There is a nice selection of sandwiches, mixing deli standards with such treats as the sheepherder — turkey or pastrami with green chile and cheese heated in a flour tortilla. The soup of the day is always delicious and the salads are good. The small space is often crowded at noon.

Continental breakfast and lunch. Closed Sunday. No cocktails. No reservations. Inexpensive. Master Card and VISA accepted.

*** The Haven. 613 Canyon Road.

The Haven may have the most unusual and varied menu in the city. There are not many choices, but the selection circles the globe in flavors. The smoked fresh trout is the closest to home and one of the best dishes. From farther away, The Haven serves lamb moussaka, East Indian curry, and Hunan stir-fried tofu, mushrooms, and vegetables, along with fresh seafood specials. It's an ambitious menu, capably handled.

The Sunday brunch is even better than dinner. The selections vary, but usually include egg dishes, smoked salmon, homemade bagels and jam, something sweet, fresh juice, and excellent coffee.

Dinner, Tuesday-Sunday, and brunch on Sunday. Closed Monday. No cocktails. Reservations advised. Inexpensive to moderate for brunch, expensive for dinner. American Express, Carte Blanche, Master Card, and VISA accepted.

* The Jefferson Company. 409 W. Water.

The breakfast is tasty and substantial. The sourdough pancakes, *huevos rancheros*, omelets, and specials are as refreshing as the recently-squeezed orange juice. The hamburgers and soups served at lunch are also good. The atmosphere is casual, the service friendly and attentive.

Breakfast and lunch. Open daily. No cocktails. No reservations. Inexpensive. No credit cards.

* La Paloma. 225 E. De Vargas.

La Paloma, located behind the "Oldest House," offers homemade pasta, soups, salads, and New Mexican dishes. The food is fresh and hearty, and is served until relatively late at night. On weekends the restaurant is open until 12:30, a startling hour for the sleepy town, and features live listening music.

Lunch and dinner. Closed Wednesday. No cocktails. No reservations. Inexpensive to moderate. Master card and VISA accepted.

*** Le Mirage. 669 Canyon Road.

Le Mirage is a distinct treat, thoroughly but unpretentiously French. Tucked away among the Canyon Road galleries, the setting is splendid, particularly in the canopied courtyard in the rear of the small adobe building. The environment and food combine to create a feeling of the south coast of France.

An appetizer or a soup is a must. Both artichoke appetizers are creamy delights, and the escargot in mushroom caps is a buttery delicacy The onion soup is authentic in its rich beef stock. The rice salad, with mushrooms and vinegar and oil, is another excellent choice.

The entrees are prepared equally well.

There is usually a good selection among veal and fish dishes, including daily specials. The *cote de porc Dijonnaise* is covered in a wonderful mustard sauce. The chicken with tarragon and tomato sauce is light and savory.

The gourmet romp continues through dessert. One specialty is a custard-filled crepe in a homemade fudge sauce, as delicious as any sweet made in the city.

Dinner only. Open daily. No cocktails. Reservations required. Expensive. Master Card and VISA accepted.

* The Ore House. 50 Lincoln, on the plaza.

Popular as a bar for good drinks and a great location, The Ore House also offers fresh seafood on some days. The rest of the menu is mainly beef, but also includes chicken and a vegetarian plate.

Dinner only. Open daily. Cocktails. Reservations advised. Moderate to expensive. Master Card and VISA accepted.

** The Palace Restaurant. Burro Alley Plaza on West Palace.

The menu is extensive and varied at The Palace, ranging from steaks to turtle soup, veal to New Mexican dishes. As usual, however, what is gained in quantity is lost in quality. Everything is handled competently, and sometimes superbly, but the range is too great for the kitchen to master consistently. The one area where the magnitude of the selection is a true asset is the wine list, which is even longer than the menu and contains some rare opportunities.

Lunch and dinner. Closed Sunday. Cocktails. Reservations advised. Moderate to expensive. American Express, Diners Club, Master Card, and

VISA accepted.

* Palace Swiss Bakery. 320 Guadalupe.

Few restaurants do better with fine baked goods than with soups and sandwiches, but the Palace Swiss Bakery is one. The pastries and breads are exceptional, making the continental breakfast an uncommon treat. The lunch menu includes pizza and quiches in addition to soups and sandwiches, all of which are reasonable excuses for getting to the divine pastries afterwards.

Breakfast and lunch. Closed Sunday. No cocktails. No reservations. Master Card and VISA accepted.

* Pasqual's. 121 Don Gaspar.

A small, downtown restaurant, Pasqual's offers a broad range of selection at both breakfast and lunch. The breakfast menu features *huevos rancheros* as well as standard egg and pancake dishes. For lunch there are a few regional dishes, plus sandwiches, soups, Chinese food, and good desserts. The Sunday brunch maintains the variety and is served from an early hour.

Breakfast and lunch. Open daily. No cocktails. No reservations. Inexpensive. American Express, Master Card, and VISA accepted.

**** The Periscope. 221 Shelby.

The best meal in Santa Fe is available only on Saturday nights. The Periscope's chef-owners, Joe and Shirley Pisacane, prepare fine lunches on Tuesday through Friday and then let loose on Saturday dinner. On these weekly occasions they strive to create as complex and satisfying a meal as any being served that night in the United States, and succeed with some regularity. It is a seven-course dinner, moving from hors d'oeuvre to appetizer, soup, sherbet, a choice of three entrees, then salad and dessert. It is always marvelous and sometimes sublime. Reservations should be made as far in advance as possible, particularly in the summer.

The lunch menu changes daily and ranges as far around the world as the Saturday dinners. There are usually five or six entrees, an appetizer, soup, and desserts. Everything is prepared with genuine attention to detail.

Lunch Tuesday-Friday, dinner on Saturday. Closed Sunday and Monday. Cocktails. Reservations required. Moderately priced for lunch, expensive for dinner. No credit cards.

***The Pink Adobe. 406 Old Santa Fe Trail.

Rosalea Murphy's gourmet menu is one of the most unusual in town and certainly the best balanced between New Mexican and other styles of cooking. Her local specialties — such as the chicken enchiladas with green chile and sour cream — are as good as those served anywhere, and the non-regional dishes are equally well made.

Among the appetizers on the dinner menu, the shrimp remoulade is very good, though the Creole entrees are not quite up to par with the other selections. The steaks are very good — especially the Dunnigan, with green chile, and the tournedos — as is the *porc Napoleone* and the *poulet Marengo.* Lunches feature a larger number of New Mexican dishes, along with sandwiches and salads. The apple pie, served with a rum sauce, is superb.

The restaurant's Dragon Room bar, next door, is a cozy place for a drink before or after dinner. In contrast with the old Santa Fe mood in the restaurant, the bar is in a new passive-solar building, bright and lively.

Lunch, Monday-Friday, and dinner daily. Cocktails. Reservations advised for lunch and required for dinner. Moderate to expensive. American Express, Diners Club, Master Card, and VISA accepted.

** Shohko Cafe. 321 Johnson.

The pleasant Japanese milieu is quite a change for Santa Fe, but the Shohko Cafe proves that it belongs in the city by offering what must be the only green chile tempura in the world. The selection in the sushi bar is more traditional, with tuna, eel, squid, and octopus, which can be ordered as appetizers or as an entire meal. Entrees, which are served with soup, salad, and rice, include sukiyaki, teriyaki, and tempura specialties.

Lunch and dinner. Closed Sunday, except in the summer. No cocktails. Reservations advised. Moderately priced. Master Card and VISA accepted.

** The Steaksmith. 210 Don Gaspar.

The Steaksmith is the first choice of most residents for steaks. The beef is good, is cooked precisely to order, and is fairly priced. The seafood is also prepared well, and the salad bar is fresh and complete. The small lounge, near the entrance, has more atmosphere than the restaurant, but the setting is comfortable throughout.

Dinner only. Closed Sunday. Cocktails. Reservations advised. Moderate to expensive. American Express, Master Card, and VISA accepted.

* Tinnie's Legal Tender.

Located about twenty miles south of Santa Fe,

near the railroad junction in Lamy, the Legal Tender is one of a small chain of steak and seafood restaurants operated by Tinnie's in opulently-restored 19th century buildings. The decor is authentic frontier Victorian.

Appropriately enough for an old saloon, the drinks are substantial. The steaks, lobster, trout, quail, and lamb chops are all good, and the salad bar is ample.

Dinner only. Open daily. Cocktails. Reservations advised. Expensive. American Express, Master Card, and VISA accepted.

*** Victor's Ristorante Italiano. 423 W. San Francisco.

If one wants to fill up Italian style, Victor's is the place to go. The menu includes antipastos, homemade pastas, and a variety of meat dishes, served with soup and salad. Victor's antipasto plate is a delicious starter. *Braciole Falso Magro* is an unusual entree for Santa Fe — beef stuffed with prosciutto ham, egg, and pine nuts, braised in a wine sauce. The pastas are made with skill and dedication.

Victor is omnipresent in his attractively-renovated adobe, surveying response in the dining rooms, visiting the kitchen, joining conversations in the pleasant bar. You can tell he cares about his food and service.

Dinner only. Open daily. Cocktails. No reservations. Moderately priced. American Express, Master Card, and VISA accepted.

** The Winery. Galisteo at Water.

The Winery is primarily a wine, cheese, and gourmet food shop, but also serves good lunches. The menu includes a *pate* plate, a large Greek salad, several fine sandwiches, and nice house wines.

The shop has the biggest selection of wines in the city. Mr. Bottle, in the Inn at Loretto, is competitive with The Winery in quality labels, but not in the range of choices.

Lunch only. Closed Sunday. No cocktails. No reservations. Inexpensive to moderate. Master Card and VISA accepted.

Hotels

Many Santa Fe hotels and motels attempt to reflect local styles to some degree in architecture, furnishings, and food. When their efforts are successful, they help visitors to experience the distinctive character of the city. An adobe fireplace in a room, painted furniture in the Hispanic folk style, or a good green chile omelet in the morning, all contribute to a sense of the environment.

The native features of Santa Fe's inns are noted in the descriptions below. Visitors seeking the full experience should try to stay in places which are comprehensive in their embrace of local styles. It is sometimes difficult, though, to get reservations in these hotels and motels, especially in the summer, and there are good alternatives in all budget categories.

The ratings are based on the comfort of accommodations and the range of amenities provided. Most places have such expected conveniences as television and swimming pools. Prices quoted are for 1982. There are four categories in the rating system:

**** A four-star rating indicates one of the best inns in the country, a gracious establishment with a variety of special services.

*** A three-star hotel provides fine lodging and a significant number of amenities. Rooms are either attractively Southwestern or modern, spacious, and comfortable.

** Two stars designate a place with standard

accommodations and services, more than adequate for most travelers.

* One star indicates a good place to stay if a visitor doesn't want to pay for frills.

* Alamo Lodge. 1842 Cerrillos. (505) 982-1841.

The plain but adequate rooms tend to be small, though large family units are available. The grounds are pleasant even without a swimming pool.

Singles and doubles both start at $23.

**** The Bishop's Lodge. Tesuque. (505) 983-6377.

There is a lovely passage in Willa Cather's *Death Comes for the Archbishop* when the prelate is retiring from his duties in Santa Fe. He and a long-time companion ride north from the city on horseback, up the big hill which separates Santa Fe from the Tesuque Valley. At the top of the hill they part, the companion returning to town and the Archbishop continuing on to his retirement estate in the valley. This beautiful inn was his destination.

At the time, Bishop Lamy had only a small adobe house and a chapel on the land. After his death Joseph Pulitzer bought the property and built two large summer homes for his daughters and their families. When the family of Jim Thorpe purchased the place in 1918, they left the chapel as it was when the Archbishop died and converted the summer homes into two of the resort's luxurious lodges.

Luxury in this case is thoroughly New Mexican. Many of the rooms have log *vigas* for ceilings and small corner fireplaces, used on chilly mountain nights even in the summer. All of the spacious rooms are Southwestern in decor.

The Lodge has its own stables and over a thousand acres of riding trails. There are five tennis courts, with a resident professional and pro shop, and a trap and skeet shooting range with expert instruction. The swimming pool is located pleasantly in the center of activity and is supplemented by a whirlpool bath and saunas.

In the summer there is a special children's program included in the rates. Kids from four to twelve are picked up early in the morning for a day of supervised play, and are entertained again in the evenings with puppet and magic shows.

Summer rates also include three meals a day. The food is not the main reason for staying at the Lodge, but the breakfast and lunch buffets are ample and the dinner is a five-course meal. There are occasional New Mexican specialties, but the food is generally a combination of American and continental. Many locals frequent the restaurant because of its superb setting and the wide range of buffet selection.

The resort is located about three miles north of the Santa Fe plaza on Bishop's Lodge Road. March through May and after Labor Day, rates start at $54 for a single and go up to $143 for a deluxe suite for two. In June, July, and August the cost for the same accommodations is $82 and $190, but includes three meals and the services of the children's program. The Lodge is closed from November through February.

** Desert Inn. 311 Old Santa Fe Trail. (505) 982-1851.

The Desert Inn offers the conveniences of a motel located downtown. The rooms have all the comforts and furnishings standard for good motels anywhere, and are a short walk from the plaza.

The Prime Rib Room serves generous portions of food and drink. The menu features beef but also includes seafood and a salad bar.

Singles start at $57 and doubles at $63 in the summer. Suites are $75.

*** El Rey Motel. 1862 Cerrillos. (505) 982-1931.

El Rey Motel is the best bargain in town for Santa Fe charm. If it were located downtown, instead of on motel row, the prices would double at least.

The rooms face a large, open courtyard, nicely designed with a fountain, tiles, brick, and low adobe walls. Each of the rooms is individually decorated. Many have Indian rugs, carved furniture, and tile murals, and some come with adobe fireplaces and exposed *vigas*. There is a unit of passive-solar rooms which have patios overlooking a garden and the heated pool, and some large apartments with kitchens.

Rates vary during the year, but are always inexpensive for the atmosphere and service. In mid-summer a double is $35 and singles are several dollars less. The solar garden unit is more expensive.

*** Hilton Inn. 100 Sandoval. (505) 988-2811.

The Hilton in Santa Fe is much like Hiltons elsewhere, comfortable and commodious with all of the modern conveniences and services. There are Southwestern features in some aspects of the design and decoration, but the emphasis is on the satisfaction of usual expectations. The rooms are spacious, quiet, and well appointed.

Cassidy's restaurant and lounge are known

locally for ample servings and reasonable prices. The dinner menu includes beef, veal, and seafood, prepared well. The bar is a popular gathering spot, particularly during happy hour.

The hotel is located a few blocks west of the plaza. In the summer rates start at $60 for a single and $70 for a double, and can go up another $20 in both categories depending on views. Between mid-October and mid-June, the prices drop over $20 a room.

*** The Inn at Loretto. 211 Old Santa Fe Trail. (505) 988-5531.

The Inn is named for the historic spot it occupies, the old Loretto Academy, established in the 1850s by Bishop Lamy and the Sisters of Loretto. The hotel bought the property with the provision that it would preserve the lovely chapel which had served the school. When the hotel was completed in 1975, it became an instant city landmark, the largest and most distinctive building in a Spanish Pueblo style that has been constructed in the city in recent years.

The Inn employed local artisans to do many of the decorative details for the new hotel. The large lounge, which often has entertainment, was built with heavy carved beams. The rooms are Southwestern in flavor, with fireplaces in some instances, but modern in furnishings and comfort. The restaurant offers both New Mexican and American food. Although the hotel is only one block from the galleries of the plaza, guests can also shop on the premises in several fine stores.

Rooms are $69-74 for a single and $79-84 for a double in the summer, and slightly less from November to March.

*** The Inn of the Governors. 234 Don Gaspar. (505) 982-4333.

Located close to the state capitol, The Inn of the Governors is a few blocks south of the plaza. The accommodations are attractive and comfortable, combining Southwestern decor with modern furnishings. Many of the rooms have fireplaces.

The Inn is known among residents for good entertainment. The Cabaret presents the most exciting jazz in the city, booking nationally-prominent musicians about once a month. In between touring engagements the club features local bands, usually rock or rhythm and blues. The Forge lounge, a rustic spot with a large fireplace, also offers music, generally individual artists. In the Forge restaurant, which serves continental and American food primarily, diners can eat indoors or on a pleasant patio with another huge fireplace.

In the summer standard rooms start at $50 for a single or a double. Rooms with fireplaces are $15 extra. The rates drop from mid-October to mid-June.

*** La Fonda Hotel. 100 E. San Francisco, on the plaza. (505) 982-5511.

An inn called La Fonda was well established on this site before the opening of the Santa Fe Trail. At the time of the American occupation in 1846, the inn became the U.S. Hotel, where guests paid $1 a day for room and board, but sometimes had to sleep on and under the billiard tables in the lobby when the town was crowded.

The present building dates from 1920, though it has been enlarged several times since then. It was planned and designed by a group of local investors to reflect the historical traditions of the city in architecture and furnishings. The investors fell short of money, however, and sold the property to the Fred Harvey Company, one of the earliest large-scale promoters of Western tourism. For several decades La Fonda became the grand station for tours of the Pueblo country, before the area was readily accessible to individual motorists. Elegant dinners were served in the evening to affluent guests, while Indians danced in the lobby. Locally owned again, the atmosphere is now more reflective of local informality than of grand touring.

Many of the rooms are thoroughly Santa Fe in decor, with Spanish colonial furniture, beamed ceilings, and adobe fireplaces. The restaurant, La Plazuela, serves New Mexican specialties at every meal, along with other choices, in a beautiful enclosed courtyard. The lounge is usually a busy gathering spot, particularly when there is music. There is also a shopping arcade, a newstand which specializes in Southwestern books, and a heated swimming pool.

The summer rates start at $64 for a single and $74 for a double and drop slightly in the winter.

** Lamplighter Motel. 2405 Cerrillos. (505) 471-8000.

The rooms are standard in appearance and furnishings, though the enclosed pool and the jacuzzi are nice extras at the Lamplighter. Services include coffee in the room, a restaurant and cocktail lounge, and a package store.

Rates start at $31 for a small double and go up to $65 for a two-room suite.

*** La Posada. 330 E. Palace. (505) 983-6351.

La Posada is closer in style and appearance to the Tesuque resorts than any of the other downtown hotels. The rooms are spread out over six landscaped acres near the plaza.

Although each of the rooms is different, and some are fairly conventional, many of them are romantically Southwestern. The *casitas* have adobe fireplaces, exposed *vigas*, and skylights, and are decorated with Indian rugs and hand-painted tiles.

The center of the complex is the Staab House, a Victorian mansion built in 1882, where the restaurant and lounge are located. The restaurant serves an excellent breakfast, with both New Mexican and American specialties, and has the best salad bar in the city for lunch. The elegant Victorian lounge, with overstuffed chairs, crystal chandeliers, and leather bar stools, is one of the most popular bars in town. In warm weather both drinkers and diners can move outside to a lovely courtyard.

The least expensive rooms start at $35 for a single and $40 for a double. *Casitas* range from $64 to $210, depending primarily on the number of bedrooms.

* Motel 6. 3007 Cerrillos. (505) 471-2442.

Motel 6 has the least expensive rates in town for a minimum level of comfort. Singles go for $14.45, doubles for $18.45, and four people can squeeze in a room for $21.45.

*** Preston House. 106 Faithway Street, off E. Palace. (505) 982-3465.

The Preston House is a British-style bed and breakfast inn located in an historic home a few blocks from the plaza. George Preston, the law partner of a notorious land speculator, built the house in 1886.

The only surviving example of Queen Anne architecture in the city, the house reflects popular local tastes of Preston's time, when native adobe styles were out of fashion. In the 20th century, when interest in adobe revived, the brick facade was covered with stucco.

The five tastefully-furnished rooms vary considerably in price. One is available with a shared bath for $35, while two others with fireplaces and private baths go up to $95. The rates, which include a continental breakfast, are slightly lower in the winter and for stays of one week or longer.

** Ramada Inn. 2907 Cerrillos. (505) 471-3000.

The Ramada provides accommodations and services similar to Ramadas everywhere. The Coach Room menu features New Mexican dishes, steaks, and a salad bar at moderate prices. The adjoining bar usually has live entertainment.

Singles in the summer begin at $34. Extra adults beyond that are $7 each.

**** Rancho Encantado. Tesuque. (505) 982-3537.

The "Enchanted Ranch" is about eight miles north of Santa Fe, in the same valley that houses The Bishop's Lodge and the small village of Tesuque. The Rancho spreads out across rugged, nicely-landscaped hills which afford a grand view of the Jemez Mountains and the sunset. The enchanted setting has enticed such guests as Princess Grace and Prince Rainier of Monaco, Nelson Rockefeller, Maria Callas, John Wayne, and Robert Redford.

The 24 rooms of the intimate inn are the most attractive overall of any accommodations near Santa Fe. All of the rooms have exposed *vigas* and are decorated in traditional Southwestern style, with Indian rugs, hand-painted tiles, and no T.V.s. Most have adobe fireplaces and a stacked supply of fragrant pinon pine.

Hostess and owner Betty Egan emphasizes gracious service at the Rancho, but also provides all of the outdoor activities anyone could desire. There are escorted trail rides into the Sangre de Cristo Mountains, a hill-top swimming pool, tennis courts, archery, and more.

The restaurant is a favorite of Santa Fe residents, particularly when they are going to the Opera, only minutes away. The dinner menu includes chicken enchiladas, steaks, and trout. The best meal, though, is breakfast. The *huevos rancheros,* other egg dishes, and pancakes are delicious. All of the meals are served with wonderful views from either the front patio or the inside dining room.

From April through October rates in the main lodge start at $95. A *casita,* with living room, is $145 and the luxury suites are higher. Rates are lower in November and December. The Rancho closes shortly after the beginning of the new year until the first of April.

** Rodeway Inn. 2900 Cerrillos. (505) 471-8072.

At the Rodeway Inn comfortable but standard rooms line the large heated pool. A popular New Mexican restaurant, Raul's, has relocated here from downtown, adding an element of local character.

In the summer singles start at $39 and doubles at $46.

** Santa Fe Inn. 3011 Cerrillos. (505) 471-1211.

The rooms and the food at the Santa Fe Inn are fairly standard, but the sauna and therapy pool are nice extras. The lounge is an active spot which usually has live entertainment.

Summer rates are $40 for a single and

$45-50 for a double.

*** Sheraton Inn. 750 N. St. Francis. (505) 982-5591.

The Sheraton is situated on a hill overlooking the old section of Santa Fe, about two miles from the plaza. It resembles other Sheratons in comfort and services, but is Spanish in many aspects of architectural design. The rooms are large and modern and some have excellent views of the city and the Sangre de Cristo Mountains.

The views are also good from the restaurant and Lookout Lounge. The restaurant offers a varied menu, including New Mexican dishes, and features a big Sunday buffet brunch. There is often music in the lounge and dancing at the Top of the Hill Club.

For guests without cars, the hotel operates a convenient limousine service to and from town. In the summer rates start at $63 for a single and $73 for a double, and go up a few dollars for better views. In the winter prices for the same accommodations are $47 and $57 respectively.

* Stage Coach Motor Inn. 3360 Cerrillos. (505) 471-0707.

Set in a spacious courtyard and picnic area, the Stage Coach has more exterior local charm than most motels in its neighborhood and price category. The rooms are a reasonable size, but the furnishings are a little spartan.

Rooms with one bed start at $26.

*** Sunrise Springs Inn and Conference Center. La Cienega. (505) 471-3600.

Sunrise Springs was developed in recent

years as a center for natural healing. Although it is open to anyone, it features a variety of health-oriented amenities. There is a ceremonial sweat-lodge, a large hot tub, professional massage, classes in yoga and meditation, as well as swimming and boating in a spring-fed pond, volleyball, and a jogging track. The retreat is located on 33 rural acres in La Cienega, about 15 minutes south of downtown Santa Fe.

Accommodations range from inexpensive dormitory space to beautiful suites. Some of the rooms are in a turn-of-the-century farm house. Others are in attractively-designed, recent buildings constructed with traditional local materials. Many have adobe fireplaces or wood-burning stoves, refrigerators, a wet bar, and patios or balconies. Rates start at $10 in the dormitory and go up to $150 for some suites, with breakfast. There are special weekend rates in the winter which include all meals.

* Thunderbird Inn. 1821 Cerrillos. (505) 983-4397.

The rooms are pleasant and clean, though some are very small. There is a heated swimming pool, but no restaurant.

In the summer singles are $30 and doubles start at $32. Three-room family units, sleeping up to 12 people, are also available. After the summer the rates drop about $10 a room.

* Travelodge. 646 Cerrillos. (505) 982-3551.

The closest of the Cerrillos Road motels to the center of town, the Travelodge is moderately convenient and moderately priced. There is no restaurant, but good choices are nearby. The rooms are standard for the chain.

In the middle of the summer a single is $38

and a double is $46. The rates drop at other times of the year.

* Warren House. 3357 Cerrillos. (505) 471-2033.

The Warren House is a budget alternative for stays of one week or longer. Rooms can be rented by the night — $27 for a single and $32 for a double — but units with kitchens are available at good discounts for extended visits.

Nightlife

No one visits or lives in Santa Fe because of its nightlife. When the gambling halls closed early this century, and the *fandango* went out of fashion, a big gap was left in local entertainment. Performing arts events fill the void for a couple of months, but the rest of the year is fairly lean.

Most residents do their socializing in homes or cars instead of clubs. High school students and other young adults frequently find diversion in low-riding, driving very slowly along certain favored streets in long lines in both directions, checking out the passengers in on-coming cars and occasionally stopping the line to chat awhile in the middle of the street. Most local preppies don't do anything so gauche or inventive, but other students seem to enjoy low-riding in droves. Their parents, who can get very frustrated if they get caught in one of the long, slow-moving lines, tend to stay home with friends, books, or the T.V.

Anyone with determination, however, can find other forms of amusement at any time of the year. Santa Fe is not as slow or straight-laced as most cities of its size. The range of choices may be narrow, but the options available are often lively.

The performing arts

Most of the action is at performing arts events. The summer festivals and other occasional events during the rest of the year offer exciting entertainment and attract the largest crowds in the city.

In addition to the festivals, described in an

earlier chapter, another important summer event is Maria Benitez's performance season at El Gancho Restaurant. A native of Taos who performs in New York most of the year, Benitez is probably the best flamenco dancer in the country. She and her accompanists dazzle audiences with their footwork, guitar playing, and lusty enthusiasm. They perform in dinner shows most nights of the summer and in late-night shows, without dinner, on weekends.

During the rest of the year there are a variety of other professional and community performances in Santa Fe. The Orchestra of Santa Fe, which produces the Bach Festival in February, plays a series of concerts during the fall, winter, and spring. The Santa Fe Community Theater operates a year-round season. Ad hoc groups of professionally-trained dancers, theater artists, and musicians frequently come together to produce a special event, usually involving new or experimental work. These performances are often staged at the Armory for the Arts or the Greer Garson Theatre at the College of Santa Fe, both of which also present touring shows. The Cabaret, downstairs at the Inn of the Governors, brings in nationally-prominent jazz artists about once a month.

Hot tubs

One of the most unusual diversions in Santa Fe is soaking in a hot tub. There are two attractive places in the city to try it. Both offer therapeutic massages in addition to the tubs, but neither is a massage parlor fronting for other thrills.

The Soak, located downtown at 207 E. Lincoln, has private rooms with tubs, showers, stereo music, blow dryers, and beds. Some of the rooms include a sauna and others have outdoor tubs. The Soak also serves soups, sandwiches, and salads either in the room or in the foyer restaurant. It is almost the only place to eat downtown late at night.

Ten Thousand Waves is a Japanese bathhouse in the mountains, about three and a half miles from the plaza up the road to the Ski Basin. Patrons don kimonos and sandals in the dressing area before going to their assigned tub, all located outside. There is one communal tub, for up to 12 people, and seven private tubs with different views of the sunset and stars. Bathing suits are provided for the shy.

An entirely different soaking experience is available in Ojo Caliente, a small town about an hour north of Santa Fe. The main business in the town is an old, slightly run-down spa built around natural hot springs. The separate facilities for men and women both feature mineral water pools, arsenic baths, and sweat tables. It's a different era of soaking, an interesting return to Victorian styles of health care. The spa is not open at night, but can wash away painful memories of the evening before.

Dancing

The best-known dance bands playing in the Santa Fe area are usually at The Line Camp or The Golden Inn, both of which feature live country or rock music on weekends. The Line Camp is in Pojoaque, about 15 miles north of Santa Fe. The Golden Inn is farther from the city in the opposite direction on N.M. 14.

Several hotels and bars in town also have live music and dancing, mainly on weekends. La Fonda Hotel, Sheraton Inn, Inn of the Governors, Inn at Loretto, Ramada Inn, and Santa Fe Inn are good bets among the hotels. The Ore

House, on the plaza, alternates between live and recorded music in a variety of styles on different nights of the week. Alfonso's Restaurant (724 Canyon Road), the Bull Ring (414 Old Santa Fe Trail), Jimmy's-Tiny's (St. Francis at Cerrillos), the Three Thieves Restaurant (I-25 Frontage Road), the Natural Cafe (1494 Cerrillos), and the Palace (Burro Alley Plaza) tend toward mellow sounds. The Office (1611 Calle Lorca), De Arcos Lounge (3397 Cerrillos), the Turf Club (6800 Albuquerque Highway), the Theater Arts Corporation Club (905 St. Francis), and the Lone Butte Saloon (on N.M. 14 south of town), usually go for a heavier beat and more dancing.

The Senate Lounge (221 Galisteo) has recorded disco music most nights of the week. The clientele is primarily gay but is friendly to straights who aren't offended by loose and lascivious dancing. The same is likely to be true of the disco at 123 W. San Francisco, though it has been in flux and could change its orientation. On costume occasions, such as Halloween, these are the places for fun.

Bars

Because of New Mexico liquor laws, almost all of the bars in Santa Fe are attached to a restaurant, hotel, or dance floor. One of the few exceptions is Evangelo's (200 W. San Francisco), which offers a pool room instead.

The best places for conversation, without music or dancing, are at La Posada Inn (330 E. Palace), El Farol (808 Canyon Road), The Pink Adobe (406 Old Santa Fe Trail), Cassidy's (in the Hilton), Victor's (423 W. San Francisco), El Nido (Bishop's Lodge Road in Tesuque), and the Rancho de Chimayo (in Chimayo).

The horses

The thoroughbreds and quarter horses at the Santa Fe Downs don't run at night, but the track is a good place to get an early jump on the evening. The season is from May until September.

Films

In addition to conventional movie theaters, Santa Fe has two alternative cinemas and a non-profit media center. The Collective Fantasy (418 Montezuma) and City Lights (St. Francis at Cerrillos) show foreign and classic films nightly. The Rising Sun Media Arts Center, located in the Armory for the Arts, sponsors various film series with different themes, focusing on experimental and artistically-significant work.